Sto

Date Due

WORSHIP AIDS
FOR
52 SERVICES

WORSHIP AIDS
FOR
52 SERVICES

Edited by
FRIEDRICH REST

Philadelphia
THE WESTMINSTER PRESS

PRINTED IN THE UNITED STATES OF AMERICA

PREFACE

765835

The needs of a leader of worship and an attempt to meet those needs can be told simply by giving the background of this book.

Facing the sacred task of leading others in the worship of God, I found myself wishing again and again that outstanding materials available in many books could be selected and organized conveniently into one book. The desire became more intense each time I prepared for a meeting or a church service where I had responsibility in leading others in the worship of God. I began to organize my notes of suitable worship aids for various occasions. The plan that appealed to me most was to have the worship aids grouped according to the type of service, so that Christmas worship aids, for instance, could be found on two or three successive pages. Care was taken to obtain what I thought were the best aids for each service.

After the material was organized and typed for the first time, I asked several interested clergymen of denominations other than my own to use carbon copies of these aids for a year as they conducted worship in their churches. Rev. Edward H. Hammon, Rev. Kermit Olsen, and Rev. Samuel Martin were helpful. The book was in a constant state of revision over a period of seven years as the material was tested in city, town, and open country churches. In conversation with me about the book, others, whom I will name in the acknowledgments, also gave encouragement and worthy suggestions.

For further help it was thought advisable to have several authorities in the field of worship give sympathetic and critical attention to the worship aids selected and revised.

The following were asked to look over the manuscript: Dr. Deane Edwards, Executive Secretary of the Commission on Worship of the Federal Council of the Churches of Christ in America, now merged in the National Council of the Churches of Christ in the U. S. A.; Bishop Ivan Lee Holt, chairman of the Commission for the Methodist *Book of Worship for Church and Home* and chairman of one of the committees that brought to completion *The Methodist Hymnal;* and Dr. Purd E. Deitz, who was Professor of Practical Theology at Eden Theological Seminary before his election to the Secretaryship of the Board of National Missions of the Evangelical and Reformed Church.

Many suggestions made by those who examined the manuscript have been incorporated; obviously, however, no one but myself is to be held responsible for whatever shortcomings this volume may have.

This book seeks to present in convenient form for leaders of worship the following worship aids in each of the units included:

The Name of the Sunday or Day
The Range of Dates in Which the Sunday Is Observed
The Liturgical Color of the Day
An Opening Sentence, or a Call to Worship
An Invocation
Scripture Lesson References, with Descriptive Titles
A Full General or Pastoral Prayer, with Paragraph Headings
An Offertory Sentence and an Offertory Prayer.

Where it was thought to be helpful or suggestive, the following material was added:

A Prayer for the Choir
A Collect
An Alternate Opening Sentence
An Alternate Invocation, or Invocation and Confession
An Alternate General Prayer (for Easter only)
An Alternate Offertory Sentence
Hymns for the Lenten Season
Salute to the Flags (on Independence Sunday only)
Alternate Benedictions.

At the end of the volume may be found Acknowledgments, Sources, and an Index.

To keep the volume from becoming too large, I present here selected materials that I have collected and revised for use on the most widely observed days in the time-honored Church year and also the most outstanding of newer Special Days.

The knowledge that identical or similar aids in worship for specific Sundays are being used in many churches of different denominations on the same day, and sometimes even at the same hour, could be a source of inspiration to many Christians.

While this book was created basically with the needs of a clergyman in mind, a leader in Sunday church school or other Christian organization may find abundant material to help him in his important task of leading others in vital Christian worship and devotion. I shall feel well rewarded if anyone using this book will find in it helpful suggestions for leading others in observing the Christian year and the Special Days which have arisen because of contemporary needs.

I wish that the duty and privilege of worship were so emphasized that all Christians would rejoice at the prospect of going into the house of the Lord where they have an appointment with the Most High God. Each of us may well plead: " O magnify the Lord with me, and let us exalt his name together " (Ps. 34:3).

Christian worship is the heartbeat in the body of Christ. When it pulsates in reality and beauty, it creates a deeper conviction that worship is a sacred privilege as well as a holy obligation. We rejoice that people today are beginning to magnify the corporate worship of God as the most important single activity of the Church. We are blessed in worship by the presence of Him who has promised to meet with those who gather in his name.

AN EXPLANATION OF THE WORSHIP AIDS

The object of the minister and the congregation in the church service is to participate in sincere and inspiring worship. To accomplish this high aim week after week, a beautiful church is very helpful, but vital and beautiful expressions of the heart are indispensable.

This book is based on the assumption that a systematic program of adaptable materials will help to meet the needs of modern worship. With the coming of special events and unusual needs, the leader of worship may select, add to, leave out, or revise certain parts of this book as the needs arise and circumstances demand. The ideal use of this book requires imaginative adaptation rather than slavish adherence.

It almost goes without saying that the optional aids gathered and revised from many treasuries of devotion do not crowd out the definite leading of the Holy Spirit. They are meant to be " wings " of worship, which the minister or other leader of worship is as free to use as the selected treasures in his hymnal.

The first unit of worship aids, for the First Sunday in Advent, is preceded by a section called " Constant Worship Aids." These aids are:

A. Solemn Declarations (usually used at the beginning of the service).

B. Forms for the Confession of Sins and Assurance of Pardon.

C. Affirmations of Faith.

D. The Lord's Prayer.

E. Ascriptions of Praise.

F. Benedictions.

They are grouped together at the beginning as a convenience, and are not repeated elsewhere in the book because they are suitable throughout the year.

No attempt is made in this volume to present an order of the divine worship service. For the sake of convenience, however, the following worship aids are arranged within the units in the approximate order in which they are generally used:

1. A Prayer for the Choir may be offered in their presence before they enter the church. Suggestions are frequently given for this purpose.

2. The Opening Sentence consists of a Biblical call to praise or an invitation to give thanks or a statement pertaining to the theme of the day. The effectiveness of many Opening Sentences in the various units may be enhanced by the use of one of the Solemn Declarations either before or after the Opening Sentence.

3. The Invocation seeks simply to invoke God's blessing on the service of divine worship.

4. Scripture Selections marked *A* are the ancient selections as recorded in the authorized *Book of Worship* of the Evangelical and Reformed Church. These passages, with a few exceptions which are marked in the body of this book, are the same ones used in the Lutheran and Episcopalian denominations at least, and have been hallowed by centuries of use throughout the Christian world. While the selections do not coincide with the Roman pericope, the differences are not great. Hymnals sometimes contain the complete ancient selections referred to in the units of this volume so that the worshipers may follow the words as the minister reads.

Despite all the favorable points of the ancient selections, critics have pointed out that they omit many of the Old Testament's greatest passages. For this reason we have added, when space permitted, some of the newer selections on various days in the Church year. These additions for voluntary choice generally correspond to the basic ideas in the ancient selections.

References marked *E* are the Eisenach Epistles, Gospels, and Old Testament lessons for the Sundays in the Church year. Readings marked *P* are taken from the complete lectionary in *The Book of Common Worship,* Presbyterian, originally in *The Book of Common Order* of the Church of Scotland. References marked *T* are the Thomasius selections of Epistles, Gospels, and Old Testament texts, which have been included on a few occasions. Selections marked *S,* used much less frequently in this volume than those previously mentioned, are the Synodical Conference texts, originally planned by

Rev. Frederic Soll. The letter *L* before certain lessons stands for the late Professor R. C. H. Lenski's recommendations selected from the newer lines of Scriptural passages. The letters *F. S.* will identify selections from Rev. Frederic Soll's lists, other than those in the Synodical Conference. The letter *O* simply stands for other selections, which are put down chiefly for Sundays rather new in Christian observance, such as World-wide Communion Sunday.

5. If the minister who is used to offering free or extemporaneous prayers will read prayerfully once or twice the material appropriate to his service, he will, I hope, find suggestions for the enrichment of expression. Possibly notations will be helpful in conducting the service. On the other hand, no one who uses a copy of this book in the church service should be without a fresh acquaintance with the matter at hand, or his reading may lack in vitality and depth of understanding. I think it is true that the best use of either free or read prayers presupposes careful preparation of the mind and heart. A fitting place in the General or Pastoral Prayer for additional intercessions is marked in each unit with the words "Special Intercessions." Many special prayers will be found in the body of this book on appropriate Sundays. When additions are made, it may be found especially expedient or even necessary to omit some of the printed paragraphs in the General Prayer. The minister should feel completely free to do with the parts of the General Prayer what he deems best. We notice in *A Book of Common Order* (1884 edition, Church of Scotland) that the intercessions are offered after the sermon, a suggestion which, if followed, would be one way of making the General Prayer shorter.

6. If the minister usually announces that an offering is to be given, he may state an Offertory Sentence, to give a brief stewardship emphasis from the Bible in each service.

7. The Offertory Prayers are given to dedicate substance and self in service. Where it is customary to give the prayer before the offering is brought forward, a change of tenses will be found necessary.

It may not always be desirable to use the material in this book on the occasions suggested. Many will want to combine Church Year and Special Day units, such as the Second or Third Sunday in Advent with Universal Bible Sunday. Variations are possible in a similar way for other Sundays in the year. Variety in forms for the Confession of Sins and Affirmation of Faith may be considered.

If it is true that an occasional repetition of a hymn or an anthem is meaningful and satisfying to most worshipers, it may also be true that occasional repetition of prayers would be as meaningful as new material. The index in this book contains references for adapting some of the themes to other occasions. The following list may be of interest to anyone desiring to re-emphasize certain themes more than once a year by offering them on occasions other than the ones for which they were originally selected and adapted:

For a Sunday evening in Advent: parts of units 1 to 4, on the theme of Christ's coming; unit 52, on the Universal Bible theme.

For another Christmas service: parts of units 4, 5, and 6, on the Christmas theme.

For a Third or Fourth Sunday after the Epiphany: unit 36, on divine love.

For an additional Lenten or Holy Week service: units 27 and 28, on the Passion theme; units 15, 17, 19, 21, 23, and 25, on the Passion theme.

For a Third or Fourth Sunday after Easter: units 30 and 31, on the theme of the living Christ, the Good Shepherd.

For a Children's Day service: unit 31, on the theme of the Good Shepherd.

For another Sunday in June: unit 14, on the theme of love; unit 42, on the theme of the Christian home.

For Sundays in the summer and fall: unit 9, on service and consecration; unit 10, Jesus' glory and the consecration of the family; parts of unit 35, on the Holy Trinity and God's greatness; units 37 and 38, on the channels for the flow of divine love and God's love for the lost; unit 47, missions; units 40 and 49, on social justice, brotherhood, and peace; parts of unit 52, on the Bible.

The Scriptural quotations from the *Revised Standard Version of the New Testament,* published in 1946, are marked with the letters "*R.S.V.*"; quotations from the American Standard Edition of the Revised Bible are marked "*A.S.V.*" Numerous quotations from the King James Version are familiar and not specially designated.

A somewhat liberal form of capitalization has been followed as an aid in reading. Generally, nouns and pronouns referring to God himself are capitalized as a form of respect as well.

The source of each prayer is indicated by a number in parentheses, which refers to the list of sources. The letters *ad* after a prayer indicate that the prayer has been adapted to the pattern of this book, and the letters *ab* indicate that a prayer was abridged.

The range of dates for the observance of specific Church year days, and the proper color for altar, lectern, and pulpit hangings, are placed underneath the title of each unit. The regular Church year colors are used on Special Days when no liturgical colors are appointed.

Since some of the Sundays in the year are known by several different titles, a second title is often placed in parentheses.

F. R.

St. Paul Evangelical and Reformed Church,
  Hermann, Missouri.

CONTENTS

16

CONTENTS

PART I

CONSTANT WORSHIP AIDS

A. Solemn Declarations
(or Salutations)

B. Forms for Confession

C. Affirmations of Faith

D. The Lord's Prayer

E. Ascriptions of Praise

F. Benedictions

CONSTANT WORSHIP AIDS

A. SOLEMN DECLARATIONS (or Salutations)

1. In the Name of the Father, and of the Son, and of the Holy Spirit [Ghost].

2. Grace to you, and peace, from God our Father and the Lord Jesus Christ. *Rom. 1:7.*

3. Grace be unto you, and peace, from God our Father, and from the Lord Jesus Christ. *I Cor. 1:3; Phil. 1:2.* (The first salutation given in 135.)

4. Grace, mercy, and peace, from God the Father and Christ Jesus our Lord. *II Tim. 1:2.*

5. Grace and peace be multiplied unto you, through the knowledge of God, and of Jesus our Lord. (135)

6. The Lord is in His holy temple: let all the earth keep silence before Him. *Hab. 2:20.*

7. Our help is in the Name of the Lord, who made heaven and earth. *Ps. 124:8.*

B. FORMS FOR THE CONFESSION OF SINS AND ASSURANCE OF PARDON

I

Call to Confession

Let us humbly confess our sins unto Almighty God. (126 and 128)

Confession of Sins

Most holy and merciful Father: We acknowledge and confess before Thee our sinful nature, prone to evil and slothful in good, and all our shortcomings and offenses. Thou alone knowest how often we have sinned, in wandering from Thy ways, in wasting Thy gifts, in forgetting Thy love. But Thou, O Lord, have mercy upon us, who are ashamed and sorry for all wherein we have displeased Thee. Teach us to hate our errors, cleanse us from our secret faults, and forgive our sins, for the sake of Thy dear Son. And, O most holy and loving Father, help us, we beseech Thee, to live in Thy light and walk in Thy ways, according to the commandments of Jesus Christ our Lord. Amen. (128)

Assurance of Pardon

Almighty God, who doth freely pardon all who repent and turn to Him, now fulfill in every contrite heart the promise of redeeming grace, remitting all our sins, and cleansing us from an evil conscience, through the perfect sacrifice of Christ Jesus our Lord. (128)

or this:

God so loved the world, that He gave His only-begotten Son, that whosoever believes in Him should not perish, but have everlasting life.

Hear the gracious words of our Lord Jesus Christ unto all that truly repent and turn to Him:

Come unto Me, all ye that labor and are heavy laden, and I will give you rest.

Him that comes to Me I will in no wise cast out.

The grace of our Lord Jesus Christ be with you all. Amen. (129)

II

Call to Confession

Beloved in the Lord! Let us draw near with a true heart, and confess our sins unto God our Father, beseeching Him, in the Name of our Lord Jesus Christ, to grant us forgiveness. (50 or 57)

Confession of Sins

Almighty and most merciful God our Heavenly Father: We humble ourselves before Thee, under a deep sense of our unworthiness and guilt. We have grievously sinned against Thee, in thought, in word, and in deed. We have come short of Thy glory, we have broken Thy commandments, and turned aside every one of us from the way of life. Yet now, O most merciful Father, hear us when we call upon Thee with penitent hearts, and for the sake of Thy Son, Jesus Christ, have mercy upon us. Pardon our sins; take away our guilt; and grant us Thy peace. Purify us, by the inspiration of Thy Holy Spirit, from all inward uncleanness, and make us able and willing to serve Thee in newness of life, to the glory of Thy holy Name. Through Jesus Christ our Lord. Amen. (50)

Assurance of Pardon

Hearken now unto the comforting assurance of the grace of God, promised in the Gospel to all that repent and believe: As I live, saith the Lord God, I have no pleasure in the death of the wicked, but that the wicked turn from his way and live. God so loved the world, that He gave His only-begotten Son, that whosoever believes in Him should not perish, but have everlasting life. (50)

Unto as many of you, therefore, beloved brethren, as truly repent of your sins, and believe in the Lord Jesus Christ, with full purpose of new obedience, I announce and declare, by the authority and in the Name of Christ, that your sins are forgiven, according to His promise in the Gospel. Through Jesus Christ our Lord. Amen. (50)

III

Call to Confession

Dearly beloved brethren: The Scripture moves us, in sundry places, to acknowledge and confess our manifold sins and wickedness, and that we should not dissemble nor cloak them before the face of Almighty God our Heavenly Father; but confess them with a humble, lowly, penitent, and obedient heart; to the end that we may obtain forgiveness of the same, by His infinite goodness and mercy. And although we ought, at all times, humbly to acknowledge our sins before God, yet ought we chiefly so to do when we assemble and meet together to render thanks for the great benefits that we have received at His hands, to set forth His most worthy praise, to hear His most holy Word, and to ask those things which are requisite and necessary, as well for the body as for the soul. Wherefore I pray and beseech you, as many as are here present, to accompany me with a pure heart, and humble voice, unto the throne of the heavenly grace, saying: (126)

A General Confession

Almighty and most merciful Father: We have erred, and strayed from Thy ways like lost sheep. We have followed too much the devices and desires of our own hearts. We have offended against Thy holy laws. We have left undone those things which we ought to have done; and we have done those things which we ought not to have done; and there is no health in us. But Thou, O Lord, have mercy upon us, miserable offenders. Spare Thou those, O God, who confess their faults. Restore Thou those who are penitent, according to Thy promises declared unto mankind in Christ Jesus our Lord. And grant, O most merciful Father, for His sake, that we may hereafter live a godly, righteous, and sober life, to the glory of Thy holy Name. Amen. (126)

The Declaration of Absolution or Remission of Sins

Almighty God, the Father of our Lord Jesus Christ, who desireth not the death of a sinner, but rather that he may turn from his wickedness and live, hath given power, and commandment, to His ministers to declare and pronounce to His people, being penitent, the absolution and remission of their sins. He pardoneth and absolveth all those who truly repent, and unfeignedly believe His holy Gospel. Wherefore let us beseech Him to grant us true repentance, and His Holy Spirit, that those things may please Him which we do at this present, and that the rest of our life hereafter may be pure and holy, so that at the last we may come to His eternal joy. Through Jesus Christ our Lord. Amen. (126)

IV

Call to Confession

Let us humbly confess our sins unto Almighty God. (57 and 126)

Confession of Sins

O most merciful God, who hast given Thy only-begotten Son to die for us: Have mercy upon us, and for His sake grant us remission of all our sins; and by Thy Holy Spirit increase in us true knowledge of Thee, and of Thy will, and true obedience of Thy Word, to the end that by Thy grace we may come to everlasting life. Through Jesus Christ our Lord. Amen. (57)

The Declaration of Absolution

The almighty and merciful Lord grant you absolution and remission of all your sins, true repentance, amendment of life, and the grace and consolation of His Holy Spirit. Amen. (126)

V

Call to Confession

Dearly beloved in the Lord: If we say that we have no sin, we deceive ourselves, and the truth is not in us; but if we confess our sins, God is faithful and just to forgive us our sins, and to cleanse us from all unrighteousness. Let us therefore humble ourselves before the throne of Almighty God, our Heavenly Father, and confess our manifold sins and transgressions with lowly and contrite hearts, that we may obtain forgiveness of the same, through the merits of our Lord Jesus Christ. (130)

Confession of Sins

We confess unto Thee, Almighty God, that we have sinned in thought, word, and deed. Make us truly contrite. Forgive us! And give us grace to amend our lives according to Thy Word, for the glory of Thy holy Name. Through Jesus Christ our Lord. Amen. (43)

Assurance of Pardon

Almighty God, the Father of our Lord Jesus Christ, who desireth not the death of the sinner, but rather that he may turn from his wickedness and live, and who gave His only Son to be a sacrifice for the sins of the whole world, have mercy upon you, pardon and deliver you from all your sins, confirm and strengthen you in all goodness, and bring you to life everlasting; through Jesus Christ our Lord. Amen. (130)

VI

Call to Confession

If we say that we have no sin, we deceive ourselves, and the truth is not in us. But if we confess our sins, He is faithful and just to forgive us our sins, and to cleanse us from all unrighteousness.

Let us therefore confess our sins to God, and humbly beseech Him, in the Name of our Lord Jesus Christ, to grant us forgiveness, saying: (66)

Confession of Sins

Almighty God, our Maker and Redeemer: We poor sinners confess unto Thee that we are by nature sinful and unclean, and that we have sinned against Thee by thought, word, and deed. Wherefore we flee for refuge to Thy infinite mercy, seeking and imploring Thy grace, for the sake of our Lord Jesus Christ. Amen. (57)

Assurance of Pardon

Almighty God, our Heavenly Father, hath had mercy upon us, and hath given His only Son to die for us, and for His sake forgiveth us all our sins. To them that believe on His Name He giveth power to become the sons of God, and bestoweth upon them His Holy Spirit. He that believes, and is baptized, shall be saved. Grant this, O Lord, unto us all. Amen. (57)

VII

Call to Confession

The Holy Scriptures declare that when the wicked man turns away from his wickedness and does that which is lawful and right, he shall save his soul and live.

The sacrifices of God are a broken and a contrite heart. To the Lord belong mercy and forgiveness, though we have rebelled against Him.

Let us therefore with sincere, humble, and obedient hearts, confess our sins to our Father, that we may obtain remission of the same, by His infinite goodness and mercy, saying: (66)

Confession of Sins

O God, our Heavenly Father: We have sinned against Thee, and are not worthy to be called Thy children. We have not loved Thee with our whole heart. We have not loved our neighbor as ourselves. We have not fought the good fight of faith. Unto Thee we cry: O God, have mercy upon us! Renew in us clean hearts. Through Jesus Christ our Lord. Amen. (48 and 43 ad)

Assurance of Pardon

Upon this humble confession which you have made, as a minister of the Lord Jesus Christ, and by His authority, I declare unto you, who do truly repent and heartily believe in Jesus Christ, and are sincerely determined to amend your sinful life, the forgiveness of all your sins in the Name of the Father and of the Son and of the Holy Spirit. Amen. (66)

VIII

Confession of Sins

O God, our Heavenly Father: I confess unto Thee that I have grievously sinned against Thee in many ways; not only by outward transgressions, but also by secret thoughts and desires, which I cannot fully understand, but which are all known unto Thee. I do earnestly repent, and am heartily sorry for these my offenses, and I beseech Thee of Thy great goodness to have mercy upon me, and for the sake of Thy dear Son, Jesus Christ, our Lord, to forgive my sins, and graciously to help my infirmities. Amen. (100)

Prayer for Pardon

Most merciful God, our Heavenly Father, who hast promised to hear us when we call upon Thee in the Name of Thy dear Son: Fulfill now, we beseech Thee, in every contrite heart the promise of redeeming grace; that, being delivered from our sins, cleansed from an evil conscience, and strengthened by Thy Spirit, we may pass our days in the peace of a holy life. Through Jesus Christ our Lord. Amen. (130)

IX

Confession of Sins

O Almighty God, most merciful Father: I, a poor, miserable sinner, confess unto Thee all my sins and iniquities, whereby I have ever offended Thee, and justly deserved Thy temporal and eternal punishment, but I am heartily sorry for them all, and repent of them truly; and I beseech Thee, through Thy infinite mercy and for the sake of the holy, innocent, and bitter suffering and death of Thy dear Son, Jesus Christ, to be gracious and merciful to me, a poor sinner. Amen. (100)

Assurances of Pardon

1. May the almighty and merciful Lord grant us pardon, absolution, and remission of our sins. (132)

2. The Lord God bless you now according to your faith. He hath forgiven all your sins. May He keep you in this firm assurance. Through Jesus Christ our Lord. Amen. (109)

X

Confession of Sins

Almighty God, Father of our Lord Jesus Christ, Maker of all things, Judge of all men: We acknowledge and bewail our manifold sins and wickedness, which we, from time to time, most grievously have committed, by thought, word, and deed, against Thy Divine majesty, provoking most justly Thy wrath and indignation against us. We do earnestly repent, and are heartily sorry for these our misdoings. The remembrance of them is grievous unto us; the burden of them is intolerable. Have mercy upon us, have mercy upon us, most merciful Father; for Thy Son our Lord Jesus Christ's sake, forgive us all that is past; and grant that we may ever hereafter serve and please Thee in newness of life, to the honor and glory of Thy Name. Through Jesus Christ our Lord. Amen. (126)

Assurance of Pardon

Almighty God, our Heavenly Father, who of His great mercy hath promised forgiveness of sins to all those who, with hearty repentance and true faith, turn unto Him, have mercy upon you; pardon and deliver you from all your sins; confirm and strengthen you in all goodness; and bring you to everlasting life. Through Jesus Christ our Lord. Amen. (126)

XI

Confession of Sins

O Lord God, who in Thy tender compassion didst send Thy Son to be our Saviour: Have mercy upon us. We have sinned and done amiss, and are not worthy to lift up our eyes to heaven, for we have left the way of Thy righteousness and have walked after the waywardness of our own hearts. Yet, in Thy great goodness, spare us, O Lord, and save us, for Thy Name's sake. Forgive us all our sins, and help us that we may walk in the way of Thy commandments, serve Thee faithfully in our day and generation, and finally attain everlasting life through Jesus Christ our Lord. Amen. (48 ad)

Assurance of Pardon

Our Heavenly Father: Thou hast assured us that if we confess our sins, Thou art faithful and just to forgive our sins and to cleanse us from all unrighteousness. Give us true penitence, and help us unfeignedly to believe Thy promises of pardon. Cleanse our hearts and renew right spirits within us, and give us the peace and joy of Thy forgiveness, as gratefully we look up to Thee. In Christ's Name we ask it. Amen. (48 ad)

XII

Psalm 51 (Confession of Sins)

Words of Assurance

As the heaven is high above the earth, so great is His mercy toward them that fear Him. As far as the east is from the west, so far hath He removed our transgressions from us. Like as a father pities his children, so the Lord pitieth them that fear Him. Amen. (From *Ps. 103,* in 131)

XIII

Confession of Sins

Eternal God, in whom we live and move and have our being, whose face is hidden from us by our sins, and whose mercy we forget in the blindness of our hearts: Cleanse us, we beseech Thee, from all offenses, and deliver us from proud thoughts and vain desires; that with lowliness and meekness we may draw near to Thee, confessing our faults, confiding in Thy grace, and finding in Thee our refuge and our strength. Through Jesus Christ Thy Son. Amen. (127)

Words of Assurance

Hear what comfortable words our Saviour Christ saith unto all that truly turn to Him: Come unto Me, ye that labor and are heavy laden, and I will give you rest.

Hear also the words from Saint John's Gospel: God so loved the world, that He gave His only-begotten Son, that whosoever believes in Him should not perish, but have everlasting life.

Hear also these words of Scripture: The Lord is gracious and full of compassion; slow to anger, and of great mercy.

The sacrifices of God are a broken spirit: a broken and a contrite heart, O God, Thou wilt not despise. Amen. (126 as ad in 131)

C. AFFIRMATIONS OF FAITH

I

The Apostles' Creed

I believe in God the Father Almighty, Maker of heaven and earth;

And in Jesus Christ His only-begotten * Son our Lord; who was conceived by the Holy Ghost,** born of the Virgin Mary, suffered under Pontius Pilate, was crucified, dead, and buried; He descended into hell ***; the third day He rose again from the dead; He ascended into heaven, and sitteth on the right hand of God the Father Almighty; from thence He shall come to judge the quick and the dead.

I believe in the Holy Ghost **; the holy Catholic Church ****; the communion of saints; the forgiveness of sins; the resurrection of the body; and the life everlasting. Amen.

— — — —

* "Begotten" is not used by some denominations.
** "Holy Spirit" is used in some Churches.
*** "He descended into hell" is omitted by some bodies. "Hades" is used by some instead of "hell."
**** "One holy universal Christian Church" or "Holy Christian Church" is preferred by some bodies.

II

The Nicene Creed

I believe in one God the Father Almighty, Maker of heaven and earth, and of all things visible and invisible:

And in one Lord Jesus Christ, the only-begotten Son of God; begotten of His Father before all worlds, God of God, Light of Light, very God of very God; begotten, not made; being of one substance with the Father; by whom all things were made: who for us men and for our salvation came down from heaven, and was incarnate by the Holy Ghost of the Virgin Mary, and was made man: and was crucified also for us under Pontius Pilate; He suffered and was buried: and the third day He rose again according to the Scriptures: and ascended into heaven, and sitteth on the right hand of the Father: and He shall come again, with glory, to judge both the quick and the dead; whose Kingdom shall have no end.

And I believe in the Holy Ghost, the Lord, and Giver of Life, who proceedeth from the Father and the Son; who with the Father and the Son together is worshiped and glorified; who spake by the prophets: and I believe one catholic and apostolic Church: I acknowledge one baptism for the remission of sins: and I look for the resurrection of the dead: and the Life of the world to come. Amen. (126)

III

In the Words of Saint John

We believe that God is Spirit, and they that worship Him must worship Him in spirit and in truth.

We believe that God is Light, and that if we walk in the light, as He is in the light, we have fellowship one with another.

We believe that God is Love, and that everyone that loves is born of God and knows God.

We believe that Jesus Christ is the Son of God, and that God hath given to us eternal life, and this life is in His Son.

We believe that He is the Resurrection and the Life, and that whosoever believes on Him, though he were dead, yet shall he live.

We believe that we are children of God, and that He hath given us of His Spirit.

We believe that if we confess our sins He is faithful and just to forgive us our sins, and to cleanse us from all uncleanness.

We believe that the world passes away and the lust thereof, but he that does the will of God abides forever. Amen. (By Henry D. A. Major; 48)

IV

Our Holy Faith

Minister:

Where the Spirit of the Lord is, there is the one true Church, apostolic and universal, whose holy faith let us now reverently and sincerely declare. (48)

Minister and People:

We believe in God, the Father, infinite in wisdom, power, and love, whose mercy is over all His works, and whose will is ever directed to His children's good.

We believe in Jesus Christ, Son of God and Son of Man, the gift of the Father's unfailing grace, the ground of our hope and the promise of our deliverance from sin and death.

We believe in the Holy Spirit as the Divine presence in our lives, whereby we are kept in perpetual remembrance of the truth of Christ, and find strength and help in time of need.

We believe that this faith should manifest itself in the service of love as set forth in the example of our blessed Lord, to the end that the Kingdom of God may come upon the earth. Amen. (48)

V

The Korean Creed

We believe in the one God, Maker and Ruler of all things, Father of all men; the source of all goodness and beauty, all truth and love.

We believe in Jesus Christ, God manifest in the flesh, our Teacher, Example, and Redeemer, the Saviour of the world.

We believe in the Holy Spirit, God present with us for guidance, for comfort, and for strength.

We believe in the forgiveness of sins, in the life of love and prayer, and in grace equal to every need.

We believe in the Word of God contained in the Old and New Testaments as the sufficient rule of both faith and practice.

We believe in the Church as the fellowship for worship and for service of all who are united to the living Lord.

We believe in the final triumph of righteousness, and in the life everlasting. Amen. (48)

VI

The Congregational Creed

We believe in God the Father, infinite in wisdom, goodness, and love; and in Jesus Christ, His Son, our Lord and Saviour, who for us and our salvation lived and died and rose again and liveth evermore; and in the Holy Spirit, who taketh of the things of Christ and revealeth them to us, renewing, comforting, and inspiring the souls of men.

We are united in striving to know the will of God as taught in the Holy Scriptures, and in our purpose to walk in the ways of the Lord, made known or to be made known to us.

We hold it to be the mission of the Church of Christ to proclaim the Gospel to all mankind, exalting the worship of the one true God, and laboring for the progress of knowledge, the promotion of justice, the reign of peace, and the realization of human brotherhood.

Depending, as did our fathers, upon the continued guidance of the Holy Spirit to lead us into all truth, we work and pray for the transformation of the world into the Kingdom of God; and we look with faith for the triumph of righteousness and the life ever-lasting. (48)

VII

Psalm 23

VIII

A Short Creed

I believe in the Fatherhood of God and the brotherhood of man. I believe that Christ is the Way, the Truth, and the Life. I believe in the clean heart, the unworldly mind, and the service of love that Jesus taught and exemplified. I accept His spirit and His teaching. (68)

D. THE LORD'S PRAYER (*Matt. 6:9–13*)

1. Our Father which art in heaven, Hallowed be Thy Name. Thy Kingdom come. Thy will be done in earth, as it is in heaven. Give us this day our daily bread. And forgive us our debts, as we forgive our debtors. And lead us not into temptation, but deliver us from evil: For Thine is the Kingdom, and the power, and the glory, for ever. (Some Churches use " who " instead of " which," and " on " earth instead of " in.")

2. Our Father, who art in heaven: Hallowed be Thy Name. Thy Kingdom come. Thy will be done on earth, as it is in heaven. Give us this day our daily bread. And forgive us our trespasses, as we forgive those who trespass against us. And lead us not into temptation, but deliver us from evil. For Thine is the Kingdom, and the power, and the glory, forever and ever. Amen. (126)

E. ASCRIPTIONS OF PRAISE

1. Now unto Him that is able to do exceeding abundantly above all that we ask or think, according to the power that works in us,

unto Him be glory in the Church by Christ Jesus, throughout all ages, world without end. (127)

2. Now unto Him that is able to keep you from falling, and to present you faultless before the presence of His glory with exceeding joy, to the only wise God our Saviour, be glory and majesty, dominion and power, both now and ever. (127)

3. Unto Him that loved us, and washed us from our sins in His own blood, and hath made us kings and priests unto God and His Father, to Him be glory and dominion forever and ever. (127)

4. Now unto the blessed and only Potentate, the King of Kings, and the Lord of Lords, who only hath immortality, dwelling in the light which no man can approach unto, whom no man has seen or can see, to Him be honor and power everlasting. (127)

5. Now unto the God of all grace, who hath called us unto His eternal glory by Christ Jesus, be glory and dominion forever and ever. (127)

6. And now to the Father, Son, and Holy Spirit, three Persons and one God, be ascribed by us, and by the whole Church, as is most due, the Kingdom, the power, and the glory, forever and ever. (127 ad)

7. Unto the Father, and unto the Son, and unto the Holy Spirit, be ascribed in the Church all honor and glory, might, majesty, dominion, and blessing, now, henceforth, and forever. (127 ad)

8. Blessing, and honor, and glory, and power, be unto Him that sitteth upon the throne, and unto the Lamb forever and ever. Amen. (127)

F. BENEDICTIONS

1. The grace of the Lord Jesus Christ, and the love of God, and the communion of the Holy Ghost [Spirit], be with you all. *II Cor. 13:14.*

2. The Lord bless thee, and keep thee: The Lord make His face shine upon thee, and be gracious unto thee: The Lord lift up His countenance upon thee, and give thee peace. *Num. 6:24–26.* (In some Churches " you " is substituted for " thee.")

3. The peace of God, which passes all understanding, keep your hearts and minds in the knowledge and love of God, and of His Son Jesus Christ our Lord; and the blessing of God Almighty, the Father, the Son, and the Holy Spirit, be upon you, and remain with you always. Amen. (127 ad)

PART II

WORSHIP AIDS FOR INDIVIDUAL SERVICES

A. The Church Year
B. Special Days
C. Prayers in Time of War

A. THE CHURCH YEAR

1. FIRST SUNDAY IN ADVENT (Advent Sunday)
November 27 to December 3 (155) (Fourth Sunday Before
  Christmas)
Liturgical Color: Violet or Purple

For the Choir
Serve the Lord with gladness: come before His presence with singing. *Ps. 100:2.*

O God, whose glory the countless hosts of heaven do ceaselessly
proclaim: Graciously aid us, we beseech Thee, as we seek worthily
to fulfill our ministry and service in Thy house, that in psalms and
hymns and spiritual songs we may sing and make melody unto
Thee with our whole heart. Through Jesus Christ our Lord. Amen.
(46)

Opening Sentences or Calls to Worship
1. Sing and rejoice, O daughter of Zion: for, lo, I come, and I will
dwell in the midst of thee, saith the Lord. *Zech. 2:10.*

2. O sing unto the Lord a new song: sing unto the Lord, all the
earth. Sing unto the Lord, bless His Name; show forth His salvation from day to day. Declare His glory among the heathen, His
wonders among all people. . . . For He cometh, for He cometh to
judge the earth: He shall judge the world with righteousness, and
the people with His truth. *Ps. 96:1-3, 13.*

Invocation
Almighty God, who in Thy wise providence hast made all ages
to be the highway for the coming of Thy Son: We pray that Thou
wilt prepare our hearts to receive the blessing of His presence, promised to all who sincerely gather in His Name. Make Thyself known
to us on this day in Advent. Open the eyes of our understanding,
that we may grow in the grace and knowledge of Him who came to
bring us life, and that more abundantly. Amen. (150 ad)

Scripture Selections (50, 151, 157, 128)

A — *Rom.*   *13:8–14*   High Time to Awake Out of Sleep
    Matt.   *21:1–9*   Blessed Be He Who Comes
    (Lutherans are referred to *Rom. 13:11–14;* Episcopalians, to
    Matt. 21:1–13.)

E — *Heb.*   *10:19–25*   By a New and Living Way
    Luke   *1:68–79*   The Dayspring from on High
    Jer.   *31:31–34*   The New Covenant

P — *Mark*   *13:1–13*   The Messianic Coming
    Luke   *1:1–17*   Birth of the Baptist Foretold
    Isa.   *1:1–20*   Though Your Sins Be as Scarlet

T — *Rev.*   *1:4–8*   I Am the Alpha and Omega
    Isa.   *61:1–3*   The Acceptable Year of the Lord

General Prayer (or Pastoral Prayer)

MAKE US READY

O Lord, who hast set before us the great hope that Thy Kingdom shall come on earth, and hast taught us to pray for its coming: Make us ever ready to thank Thee for the signs of its dawning, and to pray and work for that perfect day when Thy will shall be done on earth as it is in heaven. (133 ab)

WE PRAISE THEE

O God, in glory exalted, and in mercy ever-blessed: We magnify Thee, we praise Thee, we give thanks unto Thee for Thy bountiful providence, for all the blessings of this present life, and all the hopes of a better life to come. Let the memory of Thy goodness, we beseech Thee, fill our hearts with joy and thankfulness. (129 ab)

PRAYER OF HUMILITY

Let Thy beauty be upon us, O Lord, transforming our lives from what we are to that which we ought to be, uniting us in a new love, a new grace of service, and a new happiness of obedience. Make us to know that between us and Thee there is nothing but our own blindness of heart, since Thou art so near and we are often so far away. Make us one with all Thy seekers and finders, that at last we may be one with those who triumph over time and death by Thy grace. (95)

For the Church

O God, Father of all mankind: We beseech Thee to reveal Thy mercy unto all men, and in Thy great goodness to regard those for whom we intercede. (124)

We remember before Thee Thy Church throughout the world. Heal its divisions. Endow its ministers, missionaries, and teachers with the Spirit of power, that they may by word and life, and with joy and assurance, set forth the grace of the Lord Jesus; and grant unto all its people such zeal for the cause of Christ that their number may be increased daily, and Thy Kingdom advanced. (124 ad)

For Our Denomination

As for Thy whole Church on earth, so also we pray for that branch in which Thou hast joined us unto Christ; that we may know Him more truly, love Him more heartily, and serve Him more faithfully. (124)

For Others

O Lord: We beseech Thee to hear our prayers: (124)

For all who serve Thee in any charge or office, that by Thy continual help they may be able to please Thee in all that Thou hast granted them to do. (124 ab)

For our homes, that each may be a shelter from sin and care; and for those who carry the burden thereof, that by reason of Thy abundant mercies they may still praise Thee. (124)

For the children, that they may remember Thee in the days of their youth, and grow up in Thy love and fear. (124)

For the lonely, the sorrowful, the sick, and for all in distress and temptation; that Thou wilt be their Comforter and Guide, in weakness their Strength, in weariness their Rest, and in every darkness their Light and their Salvation. (124)

SPECIAL INTERCESSIONS
CONSECRATE THE ADVENT SEASON

Be pleased in this Advent season to awaken those who have strayed from Thy paths and to humble and convert those at ease in their carelessness and sins. (66 and 54)

FOR DAILY WATCHFULNESS AND PRAYER

Eternal God, to whom we are grateful for being permitted to enter upon a new Church year: Grant us the grace to pass the time of our sojourn here in daily watchfulness and prayer, patiently looking for the day of Thy coming in great power and majesty to judge the world in righteousness. Sanctify us wholly and save us from undue love of the world. (131 and 66)

DEDICATION

Since it is of Thy mercy, O gracious Father, that another day is added to our lives, we here dedicate both our souls and our bodies to Thee and to Thy service, in a sober, righteous, and godly life; in which resolution, do Thou, O merciful God, confirm and strengthen us; that, as we grow in age, we may grow in grace, and in the knowledge of our Lord and Saviour Jesus Christ. (126)

COMMUNION OF SAINTS

Almighty God, who hast brought the living and departed into one communion of saints: We give Thee hearty thanks for the grace Thou didst bestow upon Thy servants whom Thou hast called out of this world unto Thyself. Encourage our wavering hearts by their example, that we may imitate their goodness, and at last attain, with them, to the perfect fellowship of Thy heavenly Kingdom. Through Jesus Christ our Lord. Amen. (107)

Offertory Sentence and Prayer

" Every one to whom much is given, of him will much be required." *Luke 12:48, R.S.V.*

Almighty and most merciful Father, from whom comes every

good and perfect gift: We give Thee hearty thanks for all Thy mercies. Create in us a greater love for Thee, and enable us to show our thankfulness for all Thy benefits by dedicating ourselves and all that we have to Thy service. Through Jesus Christ our Lord. Amen. (42 ad)

2. SECOND SUNDAY IN ADVENT

Sometimes Universal Bible Sunday

December 4–10 (Third Sunday Before Christmas)

Liturgical Color: Violet or Purple

Opening Sentences or Calls to Worship

1. Behold, the tabernacle of God is with men, and He will dwell with them, and they shall be His people, and God Himself shall be with them, and be their God. *Rev. 21:3.*

2. Strengthen ye the weak hands, and confirm the feeble knees. Say to them that are of a fearful heart, Be strong, fear not: behold, your God will come . . . and save you. *Isa. 35:3, 4.*

Invocation

O God, who didst prepare of old the minds and hearts of men for the coming of Thy Son, and whose Spirit ever worketh to illumine our darkened lives with the light of His Gospel: Prepare now our minds and hearts, we beseech Thee, that Christ may dwell within us, and ever reign in our thoughts and affections as the King of Love and the Prince of Peace. Grant this, we pray Thee, for His sake. Amen. (116)

Collect

Blessed Lord, who hast caused all Holy Scriptures to be written for our learning: Grant that we may in such wise hear them, read, mark, learn, and inwardly digest them, that by patience and comfort of Thy holy Word we may embrace, and ever hold fast, the blessed hope of everlasting life, which Thou hast given us in our Saviour Jesus Christ. Amen. (126)

Scripture Selections (50, 151, 128)

A — *Rom.*   *15:4–13*   In Jesus Shall the Gentiles Trust

     Luke   *21:25–36*   The Judgment Day

    (Episcopalians end the Gospel with *v. 33.*)

E — *II Peter*   *1:3–11*   Great and Precious Promises

Luke	*17:20–30*	The Kingdom Within You
Mal.,	*ch. 4*	God's Judgment of the Wicked
P — *Mark*	*13:24–37*	Ye Know Not When the Time Is
Luke	*1:18–35*	Zacharias Remains Dumb. Birth of Jesus Foretold
Matt.	*25:1–13*	The Ten Virgins
T — *I Tim.*	*6:11–16*	Fight the Good Fight of Faith

General Prayer (or Pastoral Prayer)

THANKS FOR THE WORLD BELOW AND ABOVE

Most gracious God: We give Thee humble and hearty thanks for the world which Thou hast prepared for our dwelling place, for friends and kindred, for that larger home of seen and unseen followers of Thy Son, and even the disappointments which remind us that we have here no abiding city. (53 ad)

HEARERS OF THE WORD

O God, whose Word is quick and powerful, and sharper than any two-edged sword: Grant to us who are here before Thee a real reception of Thy truth in our hearts. Through Thy holy Word, which shall never pass away, teach, guide, uphold, and comfort us, that we and all Thy people may no longer be children in understanding, but grow to the stature of perfect men in Christ, to the honor of Thy Name. (50 ad)

MAKE US FIT FOR SERVICE

Draw us ever nearer to Thyself, and fit us for Thy service. Pour Thy Spirit into our hearts to prompt the most ardent devotion to Thy service, that we may render our whole life one continued chain of thanksgiving. Guide us toward paths of usefulness and lead us in Thy way. By the quickening of Thy Spirit lift our thoughts toward things true, lovely, and of good report, and grant us visions of Thy Kingdom of good will upon earth. (99 and 66)

BLESS THE WORLD

O God, for whose Spirit our world hungers and thirsts: Bless us with peace and righteousness the world over as the season of good will comes upon us. Let Thy Spirit rule among the nations, that concord and mutual service may be established, and the mind of Christ bind people with people and race with race in brotherhood. (99 ab)

For the Happiness of Others

Support all those at this season who think and plan to give happiness to others, and give them the deepest joy in their tasks. Sustain all those who must bear added burdens to provide cheer for others. Help us all to be mindful and considerate of them. Abundantly bless those in whose hearts there is little room for joy because sorrow has come to them. Grant that in the knowledge of Christ's comfort they may find the peace that knows no end. (99 ad)

Special Intercessions
Prepare Us for Thy Coming

O Lord and Saviour, who art the Judge of the living and the dead: Give us grace to cast off the works of darkness and grant us the guidance of Thy Holy Spirit that we may live in daily preparation of Thy coming. Purify us, even as Thou art pure, that in Thy eternal and glorious Kingdom, we may become like Thee. Aid us, O Lord, that at Thy second coming to judge the world we may be with those on Thy right hand who behold with joy and uplifted hands the fullness of redemption drawing nigh; and be pleased to say graciously to us: "Come, ye blessed of My Father, inherit the Kingdom prepared for you from the foundation of the world." Come, Lord Jesus; yea, come quickly. Amen. (66 and 127)

Offertory Sentence and Prayer

For what shall it profit a man, if he shall gain the whole world, and lose his own soul? *Mark 8:36.*

Accept the offerings we present to Thee, O Lord, our Heavenly Father. Grant that our sacrifices may result in our own spiritual enrichment, and that with our gifts we may yield ourselves more fully to Thy service. Help us always to become more like Thy Son, Jesus Christ, in whose Name we pray. Amen. (91 ad)

Suggestion

Full aids for an emphasis appropriate to Universal Bible Sunday may be found in unit 52.

3. THIRD SUNDAY IN ADVENT

December 10–17 (Second Sunday Before
  Christmas)
Liturgical Color: Violet

For the Choir

We come before Thy presence, O Lord, with thanksgiving and enter Thy courts with praise. Grant that we may perfectly magnify Thy Name. Through Jesus Christ our Lord. Amen. (72)

Opening Sentences

1. Prepare ye the way of the Lord, make straight in the desert a highway for our God. And the glory of the Lord shall be revealed, and all flesh shall see it together: for the mouth of the Lord hath spoken it. *Isa. 40:3, 5.*

2. Thus saith the Lord, Keep ye judgment, and do justice: for My salvation is near to come, and My righteousness to be revealed. *Isa. 56:1.*

Invocation

Eternal Father: As we worship in Thy house prepare us to rejoice as the shepherds rejoiced at the sound of the angels' song. Fill us with joy as we hear again the story of Thy love. As the Wise Men brought their gifts to the Christ-child, help us to bring the richest treasures of our devotion and lay them before Thy majesty. As seekers in the past followed the star that led them to the shrine of His birth, prepare our hearts for the fulfillment of our need, that in this hour of worship we may find Thee, and be led to life eternal. Through Jesus Christ our Lord. Amen. (150 ad)

Scripture Selections (50, 151, 128)

A — *I Cor.*	*4:1–5*	Ministers of Christ, Stewards of Righteousness
Matt.	*11:2–10*	John in Prison

E —	*II Tim.*	*4:5–8*	A Crown of Righteousness
	Matt.	*3:1–11*	Prepare the Way of the Lord
	Isa.	*40:1–8*	God Comforts His People
P —	*Luke*	*1:39–56*	Mary Visits with Elizabeth. The Magnificat
	Matt.	*13:14–52*	Parables of the Sower, the Tares, Mustard Seed, etc.
T —	*Rom.*	*2:12–16*	Who Is Just Before God?

General Prayer (or Pastoral Prayer)

Blot Out Our Transgressions

Have mercy upon us, O God, according to Thy loving-kindness; according to the multitude of Thy tender mercies blot out our transgressions. Wash us thoroughly from our iniquities and cleanse us from our sins. For we acknowledge our transgressions: and our sins are ever before us. Purge us, and we shall be clean: wash us, and we shall be whiter than snow. Create in us clean hearts, O God; and renew a right spirit within us. Cast us not away from Thy presence; and take not Thy Holy Spirit from us. (*Ps. 51*, ad)

Help Us to Make Room

Merciful God, our Heavenly Father: We praise Thee for the blessings of this sacred season. Grant us grace and heavenly wisdom that we may receive Thy Word with pure affection and bring forth the fruits of Thy Spirit. (66)

Eternal Christ: As we approach another Christmas when the world remembers Thy birth, cause us who bear Thy Name to make room for Thee in the inner chambers of our hearts. Create in us an understanding of the deep significance of Thy coming and make us responsive to all that it means to the world. (150 ad)

Come, Lord Jesus, our blessed Saviour, and manifest Thy presence among us; revive Thy languishing people. Bestow upon us the help of Thy Holy Spirit, that we may daily increase in Thy knowledge; confess, honor, and worship Thee; take up our cross and follow Thee; and always walk as the children of light. (66 and 54)

O Thou who hast founded a Church for Thyself, and hast promised to dwell in it forever: Enlighten and sanctify it, we beseech Thee, by Thy Word and Spirit; give all pastors Thy grace, that they may with joy and assurance guard and feed Thy sheep, looking to the great Bishop and Shepherd of souls. Bless all who serve Thee in Thy Church, in the care of Thy poor, in the ministry of Thy praise, and in the teaching of the young. Strengthen them in their labors; give them courage to make a good confession; and cause Thy Church to increase more and more, that every knee may bow before Thee, and every tongue confess that Jesus Christ is Lord. Amen. (129 ad)

Offertory Sentence and Prayer

For we brought nothing into this world, and it is certain we can carry nothing out. *I Tim.* 6:7.

All things are Thine, O Lord, and of Thy own have we given Thee. We thank Thee for the abundance of Thy provision for our temporal and spiritual needs. And in gratitude we make these offerings, for the glory of Him who, though He was rich, yet for our sakes became poor, that we through His poverty might become rich. Amen. (32 ab)

4. FOURTH SUNDAY IN ADVENT (Sunday Before Christmas)
December 18–24
Liturgical Color: Violet

For the Choir

O God of all goodness: Help us to praise Thee for the wonderful gift of Thy Son. Give us such happiness within that we may lead others in joyful worship. Amen. (109)

Opening Sentences

I wait for the Lord, my soul doth wait, and in His word do I hope. My soul waiteth for the Lord more than they that watch for the morning: . . . Let Israel hope in the Lord: for with the Lord there is mercy, and with Him is plenteous redemption. *Ps. 130:5-7.*

Invocation

Almighty and ever-blessed God: We thank Thee that we are permitted once again to rejoice with Thy holy Church in the season of Advent. Grant that this approach to Christmas Day may be hallowed by devout meditations. Keep the thought of Thy love bright in our hearts, that we may be joyful. Empower us with childlike expectations and simple faith to look for the coming of Thy Son into our hearts, that we may in this hour worship Thee, and in the time that follows spread peace and good will to men. Through Jesus Christ our Lord. Amen. (118 ad)

Scripture Selections (50, 151, 128)

A — *Phil.*	*4:4-7*	Rejoice in the Lord Always
John	*1:19-28*	The Baptist's Testimony
E — *I John*	*1:1-4*	Your Joy May Be Full
John	*1:15-18*	Grace for Grace
Deut.	*18:15-19*	The Prophet of God to Be Heard
P — *Matt.*	*3:1-12*	Preaching of the Baptist

Luke	*1:59–80*	The Naming of the Baptist. The Benedictus
Luke	*3:1–14*	The Preaching of John the Baptist
T — *I Cor.*	*1:26–29*	What God Hath Chosen
Luke	*1:46–55*	The Magnificat of Mary
Isa.	*2:2–5*	Christ's Kingdom Established

General Prayer

THANKS FOR JOHN THE BAPTIST

Almighty God, who by the mouth of Thy holy prophets didst proclaim the coming of the Redeemer of the whole world: We praise Thee that Thou didst send John the Baptist to prepare the way for Thy Son Jesus Christ. Grant, O God, that the voice of Thy servant in the wilderness may move the hearts of all men to prepare a highway for the Saviour of the world, that the good tidings of great joy may be brought to all men, and every tongue confess that Jesus Christ is Lord, to the praise of Thy honor and glory. (54 and 66)

PRAYER OF CONFESSION

Almighty God, our Heavenly Father, who didst cause light to shine out of darkness in the advent of our Lord Jesus Christ to take away the sins of the world: We humbly confess our transgressions and implore Thy forgiveness. We are ashamed of that within us which makes neither for good will to others nor for growth in goodness in our own lives. We beseech Thee that the Spirit of Christ may be born anew within us, and that we may glorify His Nativity with hearts of compassion, deeds of kindly service, and the spirit of good will to all mankind. (131 ab)

MAKE READY OUR HEARTS

Almighty God, who in Thy providence hast made all ages a preparation for the Kingdom of Thy Son: We beseech Thee to make ready our hearts for the brightness of Thy glory, and the fullness of blessing in Thy Son. Assist us to join the company of believers in all ages who, finding the newborn King, have gained strength for their tasks, comfort for their sorrows, and salvation for their souls. Grant that this Christmas may be for us the open door to the Holy of

Holies, where the light of Thy presence shines forevermore. (76 and 90)

ENTER, LORD JESUS

Our hearts rejoice greatly, Lord Jesus, Son of Almighty God, for Thou art He who cometh, and we look not for another. Abide with us and let Thy heavenly favor be with us. Enter into us, Thy living temples, and sanctify us wholly in body, soul, and spirit, that we may be partakers of the glory of Thy Kingdom. Grant us strength to follow faithfully in Thy footsteps, until death. (66)

FOR OUR CHRISTMAS PLANS

We commit to Thee, O God, in this silent hour, all our Christmas plans, our hopes, our daily work, our families and family reunions, our gaieties and our griefs — asking Thy blessing upon every thought and endeavor, Thy control over every enterprise, Thy spirit of love in our hearts and wisdom in our minds. (122 ad)

SPECIAL INTERCESSIONS
BE WITH OUR WAITING EARTH

God of Love, in whose providence Thy world once echoed with the heavenly songs of "Peace on earth, good will to men": Shed abroad throughout the earth Thy Spirit until ancient animosities are forgotten, and lingering prejudices disappear, and no want goes unrelieved, and all mankind bows before the Prince of Peace. Visit in Thy sympathy all who from the shadows of loneliness and sorrow look out upon joy in which they find no share, and grant to them the Christmas peace which passes knowledge. Grant the power of His Spirit to all who beneath the guise of mirth do battle with temptations which daily press them hard, and make them more than conquerors through Him who strengtheneth. (99 ab)

FOR DIVINE SUPPORT AT THE LAST

O Lord: Support us all the day long of this troublous life, until the shadows lengthen and the evening comes, and the busy world is hushed, and the fever of life is over, and our work is done. Then in

Thy great mercy grant us a safe lodging, and a holy rest, and peace at the last. Through Jesus Christ our Lord. Amen. (94)

Offertory Sentence and Prayer

Freely ye have received, freely give. *Matt. 10:8.*

O great Giver of all good and perfect gifts, who hast given us Thy Son Jesus Christ as a Babe in Bethlehem for our enlightenment and salvation: Accept these tokens of our love for Thee and Thy Son. For His sake. Amen. (109)

5. CHRISTMAS
December 25
Liturgical Color: White

For the Choir

O Father, who hast declared Thy love to men by the birth of the holy Child of Bethlehem: Help us as we enter Thy gates, to serve Thee in purity of heart, that others may worship with gladness and make room for Him in their daily life. In His Name. Amen. (38, 66, 109)

Opening Sentences

1. For unto us a Child is born, unto us a Son is given: and the government shall be upon His shoulder: and His Name shall be called Wonderful, Counselor, The mighty God, The everlasting Father, The Prince of Peace. *Isa. 9:6.*

2. Sing, O heavens; and be joyful, O earth; and break forth into singing, O mountains: for the Lord hath comforted His people. *Isa. 49:13.*

3. Blessed be the Lord God of Israel; for He hath visited and redeemed His people, and hath raised up a horn of salvation for us in the house of His servant David. *Luke 1:68, 69.*

Invocations

1. O God, who centuries ago didst bless our earth with a vision of Thy love in the form of a little Child: We beseech Thee once more to gladden us with the light that shone round about the hills of Bethlehem. Graciously grant us a true Christmas blessing as we worship. Fill our hearts with gratitude. And lead us into the Christmas peace which passes all understanding, the peace of Thy Son and our Lord. (99 ad)

2. O Almighty God, who by the birth of Thy holy Child Jesus hast given us a great Light to dawn upon our darkness: Grant, we pray Thee, that in His light we may see light to the end of our days; and bestow upon us, we beseech Thee, that most excellent gift of

love to all men, that the likeness of Thy Son may be formed in us, and that we may have the ever-brightening hope of everlasting life. Through Jesus Christ our Lord. Amen. (81 ad)

Scripture Selections (50, 157, 151)

A —	*Titus*	*2:11–14*	The Grace of God That Brings Salvation

(Episcopalians list *Titus 2:11–15*.)

	Isa.	*9:2–7*	Unto Us a Child Is Born
	Luke	*2:1–14*	The Nativity of Our Lord
	Heb.	*1:1–12*	The Dignity of the Son of God
	John	*1:1–14*	The Word Was Made Flesh
E —	*I John*	*3:1–5*	We Are Called the Children of God
	Matt.	*1:18–23*	Wondrously Born in Bethlehem
L —	*John*	*3:16–21*	The Gift of God's Son to the World
T —	*Luke*	*2:1–20*	The Birth of Jesus Christ

General Prayer

PRAISE

Almighty God and Father of our Lord Jesus Christ: Praise be to Thy Name forever and ever. With angels and archangels and all the redeemed we glorify Thee, we praise Thee, we give thanks for all Thy wonders, which Thou hast given purely out of Divine goodness and mercy without any merit or worthiness on our part. Especially do we thank Thee for Thy Gift to the world, our Lord Jesus Christ, who (as on this day) was made flesh, and dwelt among us, full of grace and truth. (54 and 66)

ENTER INTO OUR HEARTS

Glory be to Thee, Lord Jesus Christ, our Saviour, who didst become poor that we might be made rich. We thank Thee for taking upon Thyself our nature that we might become Thy followers and true children of the Father. O Lord, Jesus Christ, true God and true man: Enter into our hearts and fill us with the grace of Thy tenderness and goodness. O Thou King of the high heavens: Establish Thy rule in our hearts and save us by Thy mercy from all misery of sin. Heal the wounds of misunderstanding, jealousy, or regret, and let the gentler air of the Christmas spirit touch our lives, as though the cold of winter were touched by the kindlier breath of spring. Teach us to remember love, to forgive anger, to forget unkindness, that something of Thy beauty may be upon us, and that Thy grace may be in our hearts. Make us compassionate one toward another, merciful, tenderhearted, forgiving one another, even as Thou art compassionate toward us, forgiving our iniquities, transgressions, and sins. (66, 104, 116)

INTERCESSIONS

O Lord, our Saviour, to whom glory is sung in the highest, while on earth peace is proclaimed to men of good will: Fill all the earth with Thy glory, and let Thy light shine upon all people who still sit in darkness and the shadow of death. Bring Thy redeemed from the east and west to the blessed heritage of the saints, where with them and all the heavenly hosts we shall sing to the honor and glory of Thy holy Name. (66 and 24)

Gather all Christian rulers about Thy manger and teach them to renew allegiance to Thee, and to use new scientific powers for the welfare of mankind. Encourage all Christians to serve as messengers of peace who recognize Thee as King. Grant that on this anniversary of Thy incarnation all parents and teachers may take to heart the message that children are sacred to Thee. Cause Thy praises to be chanted from their youthful lips. O Thou who hast mercy on all those who are poor, sick, or afflicted: Refresh them with Thy comfort. Let the light and joy of this holy season enter their homes. Awaken and strengthen within them the living hope of their eternal salvation. (66 and 54)

SPECIAL INTERCESSIONS
HELP US TO CELEBRATE HIS BIRTH

Help all Thy children, Almighty and eternal God, to celebrate the memory of Jesus' birth in the right spirit. Enable us to look to Jesus with true faith and joy; to love Him as did Mary; to worship and honor Him as do the holy angels. Give us grace to grow in His knowledge and cause us to serve Him faithfully every day of the year. (66 ad)

COMMUNION OF SAINTS

O Lord Jesus Christ, who redeemest the souls of Thy servants: We praise Thee for the multitude which no man can number, who trod the way of life with a hope in their hearts which is now fulfilled; especially we thank Thee for those dear to ourselves who once shared our Christmas joy, and now rejoice with Thy saints in heaven. Keep our love for them true and steadfast, until we also receive the end of our faith, even life forevermore. And unto Thee, O Lord Jesus Christ, with the Father and the Holy Spirit, one God, be honor and glory forever and ever. Amen. (107 ab)

Offertory Sentences and Prayer

1. For God so loved the world, that He gave his only begotten Son, that whosoever believeth in Him should not perish, but have everlasting life. *John 3:16.*

2. Each one must do as he has made up his mind, not reluctantly or under compulsion, for God loves a cheerful giver. *II Cor. 9:7, R.S.V.*

O merciful God, who didst bless the whole world by the gift of Thy Son: Be pleased to accept our offering which we present to Thee with willing hearts. Bless it that others may know of Thy wonderful love, for the sake of Him whose birth we celebrate. Amen. (109)

6. FIRST SUNDAY AFTER CHRISTMAS
December 26–31
Liturgical Color: White

For the Choir
Eternal God, who didst give Thy Son while glory was sung in the highest: Prepare our attitudes and control our spirits as we make ready to enter Thy courts, that the words we sing may proceed from joyful hearts. Bless our congregation in this worship hour for Jesus' sake. Amen. (109)

Opening Sentences
1. In this the love of God was made manifest among us, that God sent His only Son into the world, so that we might live through Him. *I John 4:9, R.S.V.*
2. This is the covenant that I will make with the house of Israel after those days, saith Jehovah: I will put My law in their inward parts, and in their heart will I write it; and I will be their God, and they shall be My people. *Jer. 31:33, A.S.V.*

Invocation
O Almighty God, who by the birth of Thy holy One in the world didst give the true light to dawn upon our darkness: Mercifully assist us in our meditation and worship of Him, that being delivered from wandering thoughts and from all anxiety of spirit we may continue to see light in Thy light, to the glory of Thy holy Name. Amen. (107 ad)

Scripture Selections (50, 157, 151, 128)
A — *Gal.*   4:1–7   In the Fullness of Time, God Sent His Son
Luke   2:33–40   Simeon and Anna
(Episcopalians refer to *Matt. 1:18–25* for the Gospel.)

E — *II Cor.*	*5:1–9*	We Walk by Faith, Not by Sight
Luke	*2:25–32*	Simeon Blesses God for His Salvation
Isa.	*63:7–16*	Loving-kindnesses of the Lord
P — *John*	*1:1–18*	The Word Was Made Flesh
T — *II Tim.*	*4:3–8*	I Have Fought a Good Fight

General Prayer

PRAISE

Almighty God, Creator and Ruler of all worlds, who in the beginning didst command the light to shine out of darkness: We bless Thee that when the fullness of time was come Thou didst give the light of the knowledge of Thy glory in the face of Jesus Christ. We bless Thee, we worship Thee, we glorify Thee, we give thanks for Thy great glory, O Lord God, Heavenly King, God the Father Almighty, that by the incarnation of Thy Son Thou hast fulfilled the promise of the ages and revealed Thy love unto men. We adore Thee for the love that brought the Lord of glory down to the manger of humiliation. We praise Thee that He dwelt among us, full of grace and truth. We thank Thee for the great light that dawned through Him upon our darkness, for the saving hope which He hath kindled, and the redemption He hath purchased. We bless Thee that in Him we know Thee as our Father, and one another as Thy children, called to love and forgive and serve, as He gave example. Praise be unto Thee, O Lord God, for Thou hast visited and redeemed Thy people. (107 ad)

AT THE CLOSE OF THE OLD YEAR

O Lord, who hast been our dwelling place in all generations, who didst exist before the mountains were brought forth, or ever Thou hadst formed the earth and the world, even from everlasting to everlasting: We thank Thee for all the blessings which Thou hast granted to us during the past year. We remember the days of the year now almost gone and humbly bow in gratitude to Thee for bearing with us in patience and long-suffering. (66 ab)

HELP US TO FOLLOW

O Lord Jesus Christ, who art the Beginning and the End, the First and the Last: We would end the old and begin the new year in Thee. Enable us henceforth to abide in Thee, and let Thy words abide in us, that we may glorify Thee in good works and holy lives. Help us to lay to heart the wisdom Thou hast been teaching us, and, forgetting the things that would come between us and Thee, to look unto Thee for guidance, and follow Thee all our days. (107 ad)

O patient and loving Saviour: Let the same mind be in us which was also in Thee. Make us patient with others, as Thou hast been patient with us. Enable us to forgive others as Thou hast forgiven us. Cast out of us every unworthy fear; and help us to face the future in the courage and peace of trust in Thee, assured that Thou wilt defend us from the evil that is behind us, and give us victory over every ill that is to come. (107 ad)

TRIUMPH OVER OUR INFIRMITIES

For the new year which we are about to enter, cause Thy grace, O Almighty God, to triumph over our infirmities, and grant us inwardly such increased steadfastness that, through sunshine and storm, we may trust and not be afraid, work and not be weary, suffer and not complain. Help us to overcome all evil with patience, and to possess our souls in humility. (53 ad)

SPECIAL INTERCESSIONS
FOR THE UNIVERSAL CHURCH

Gracious Father: We humbly beseech Thee for the Universal Church. Fill it with all truth, and in all truth with all peace. Where it is corrupt, purify it; where it is in error, correct it; where anything is amiss, reform it; where it is right, strengthen and confirm it; where it is in want, furnish it; and where it is divided and rent asunder, heal it. (16 as ad in 30)

FOR THE COMING OF GOD'S KINGDOM AND UNIVERSAL PEACE

O Thou King eternal, immortal, invisible, Thou only wise God our Saviour: Hasten, we beseech Thee, the coming of Thy Kingdom upon earth, and draw the whole world of mankind into willing obedience to Thy blessed reign. Overcome all the enemies of Christ, and bring low every power that is exalted against Him. Cast out all the evil things which cause wars and fightings among us, and let Thy Spirit rule the hearts of men in righteousness and love. Establish every work that is founded on truth and equity, and fulfill all the good hopes and desires of Thy people. Manifest Thy will, Almighty Father, in the brotherhood of man, and bring in universal peace. Through the victory of Christ our Lord. Amen. (129 ab)

Offertory Sentence and Prayer

Verily I say unto you, Inasmuch as ye have done it unto one of the least of these My brethren, ye have done it unto Me. *Matt. 25:40.*

Almighty and ever-blessed God, who in the abundance of Thy goodness dost ever give us more than we desire or dare to ask: Pour forth upon us, we beseech Thee, a spirit of thankfulness, and increase in our hearts that most blessed grace of charity, which is more willing to give than to receive; and so rule our hearts that all we have may be used for Thy service. Through Jesus Christ our Lord. Amen. (116 as ad in 46)

7. NEW YEAR'S EVE AND NEW YEAR'S DAY
December 31 and January 1
Liturgical Color: White

I

Call to Worship

Minister: Praise ye the Lord. Praise ye the Name of the Lord; praise Him, O ye servants of the Lord. Ye that stand in the house of the Lord, in the courts of the house of our God,

People: Praise the Lord; for the Lord is good: sing praises unto His Name; for it is pleasant. *Ps. 135:1-3.*

Invocation (or Collect)

Almighty and everlasting God, who art more ready to hear than we are to pray, and dost give more than we desire or deserve: Pour down upon us the abundance of Thy mercy, forgiving us those things wherein we have offended against Thee, and giving us those good things which we are not worthy to ask. Through Jesus Christ our Lord. Amen. (17 as ad in 49)

General Prayer

Almighty and eternal God of heaven and earth, with whom there is no variableness nor shadow of turning: Accept, we beseech Thee, our sacrifice of praise and thanksgiving for the goodness and mercy which have followed us all our days. We especially bless Thee for deliverance from the perils and dangers of the year which is now drawing to a close. We humble ourselves before Thee, confessing and bewailing all that we have done amiss. According to the multitude of Thy tender mercies blot out our offenses. Pardon and accept us for the sake of Thy only-begotten Son, whom Thou didst send into the world to take our nature upon Him that He might redeem us for Thee by His blood. Cleanse us from our sins, and let them be buried with the closing year, to rise up against us no more. (106 ad)

Keep us mindful, O Lord, as the years of our life pass away, that the end of all things is at hand; and make us sober and watchful unto prayer. Help us to remember that we are strangers and pilgrims upon earth, and that here we have no continuing city. Teach us so to number our days that we may apply our hearts unto wisdom. Give us grace to watch and pray, since we know neither the day nor the hour when the Son of Man cometh. Help us to fight the good fight, to finish our course and to keep the faith, that there may be laid up for us a crown of righteousness. Through Jesus Christ our Lord. Amen. (106 ad)

A Prayer for Advancing Years

O God, our Heavenly Father, whose gift is length of days: Help us to make the noblest use of mind and body in our advancing years. According to our strength apportion Thou our work. As Thou hast pardoned our transgressions, sift the ingatherings of our memory that evil may grow dim and good shine forth clearly. We bless Thee for Thy gifts, and especially for Thy presence and the love of friends in earth and heaven. Grant us new ties of friendship, new opportunities of service, joy in the growth and happiness of children, sympathy with those who bear the burdens of the world, clear thought and quiet faith. Teach us to bear our infirmities with cheerful patience. Keep us from narrow pride in outgrown ways, blind eyes that will not see the good of change, impatient judgments of the methods and experiments of others. Let Thy peace rule our spirits through all the trial of our waning powers. Take from us all fear of death, and all despair or undue love of life, that with glad hearts at rest in Thee we may await Thy will concerning us. Through Jesus Christ our Lord. Amen. (28)

A Prayer at the Close of the Year

As we keep holy time, O Lord of our life, under the deepening shadows of the closing year, may we thank Thee for all that it has brought to us of mercy and truth, for the lights that have ruled our day and cheered our night, for Thy Being and our natures, for Thy providence and our faith, for Thy dear Son and the grace by which we are His disciples, for the law which upholds and the love which comforts our world. Make this passing time sacred to us for the precious thoughts of Thee which it awakens in our hearts. Bless all to whom this has been a year of bereavement, and fulfill for them Thy Word, that at evening time there shall be light. Help us all to redeem the time and to devote ourselves more entirely to Thy high and blessed service. Through Jesus Christ our Lord. Amen. (65 ad)

II

NEW YEAR'S DAY

Opening Sentences

1. Days should speak, and multitude of years should teach wisdom. *Job 32:7.*

" Behold, I have set before you an open door, which no one is able to shut." *Rev. 3:8, R.S.V.*

2. O bless our God, ye people, and make the voice of His praise to be heard. *Ps. 66:8.*

Invocation

O God of peace, our Father: We come to Thee for refuge from the noise and hurry of the world, and the oppression of selfish thoughts and fears. Deliver us from the sins which hide Thee from us, and give us of Thy peace. And, we pray Thee, grant that the Spirit who dwelt in Thy Son without measure may so dwell in us that we may worship Thee in humility and gladness and go forth with hearts made cheerful and strong by the knowledge of Thy love. Through Jesus Christ our Lord. Amen. (133 ad)

Scripture Selections (57, 151, 128)

A —	*Gal.*	*3:23–29*	All the Children of God by Faith
	Luke	*2:21*	The Circumcision
E —	*Rom.*	*8:24–32*	All Things Work Together for the Good to Those Who Love God
	Luke	*4:16–21*	The Acceptable Year of the Lord
	Ps.	*90*	Our Dwelling Place in All Generations

P —	*Phil.*	*3:7–14*	I Press On Toward the Goal
	Matt.	*6:19–34*	Seek Ye First His Kingdom
	Deut.	*11:1–17*	Ye Shall Keep His Commandments
	Ps.	*91*	He That Dwelleth in the Secret Place
T —	*Heb.*	*13:8*	The Same Yesterday, Today, and Forever
	Luke	*13:6–9*	The Parable of the Fig Tree
	Lam.	*3:22–32*	The Multitude of God's Mercies

General Prayer

THANKS FOR THE PAST YEAR

O God, who art our merciful Father in Christ Jesus our Lord: At the beginning of this new year of our pilgrimage we come before Thee with thanksgiving. We praise Thy glorious Name for the countless and unmerited mercies which Thou hast bestowed upon us during our whole life and especially during the year that has just closed. (66 ad)

HELP US IN THE NEW YEAR

O Thou who art from everlasting to everlasting, without beginning or end of days: Replenish us with heavenly grace, at the beginning of this year, that we may be enabled to accept all its duties, to perform all its labors, to welcome all its mercies, to meet all its trials, and to advance through all it holds in store for us, with cheerful courage and a constant mind. (129 ab)

We thank Thee for the new year as a page unwritten upon; help us to write our life story with a steady hand. (139)

FORGIVE AND GIVE US STRENGTH

O Thou who inhabitest eternity, and before whom the centuries pass as a watch in the night: Set us free, that with a purer purpose and a better hope we may renew our vows in Thy presence and travel in that path which shines more and more unto the perfect day of Thy heavenly Kingdom. (122, 129)

SPECIAL INTERCESSIONS
FOR OUR CHURCH

Almighty and everlasting God, who dost govern all things in heaven and earth: Mercifully hear the supplications of us Thy servants; and grant unto the people of this place all things needful for their spiritual welfare. Strengthen and confirm the faithful; protect and guide the children; visit and relieve the sick and afflicted; turn and soften the wicked; rouse the careless; recover the fallen; restore the penitent; remove all hindrances to the advancement of Thy truth; and bring all to be of one heart and mind within the fold of Thy holy Church. (125 ab)

GENERAL INTERCESSIONS

Merciful God: Be the help and comfort of all who have entered the door of the new year in poverty, distress, sickness, or in any sort of trouble. Quicken them with the Word of life and power. (66 ad)

We also pray for all officers of our Government throughout our land. Fill them with the spirit of wisdom and understanding, the knowledge and fear of Thy holy Name, that they may be faithful in the discharge of their sacred duties. (66)

FOR THE CROWN OF LIFE

Almighty and eternal God, with whom one day is as a thousand years and a thousand years as one day: Enable us to run with patience the race that is set before us, forgetting the things that are behind, and reaching for the things that are before; that so finally by Thy mercy we may obtain the crown of everlasting life. Through Jesus Christ our Lord. Amen. (122 ad)

Offertory Sentence and Prayer

Vow, and pay unto the Lord your God: let all that be round about Him bring presents unto Him. *Ps. 76:11.*

Eternal God, who makest all things new: Graciously accept these gifts and bestow Thy favor upon them that they may bring joy to many hearts and glory to Thy Name; help us to continue in Thy favor throughout the year, spending our lives in Thy service, that finally we may obtain the glory of everlasting life. Through Jesus Christ our Lord. Amen. (91, 101, 131)

8. SECOND SUNDAY AFTER CHRISTMAS (First Sunday After New Year's Day)

January 2–5

Liturgical Color: White

Opening Sentences

1. If any man be in Christ, he is a new creature: old things are passed away; behold, all things are become new. *II Cor. 5:17.*

2. And He who sat upon the throne said, "Behold, I make all things new. . . . I am the Alpha and the Omega, the beginning and the end." *Rev. 21:5, 6, R.S.V.*

Invocation

Almighty God, our Father, who hast planted eternity in the heart of man and hast ordained that he should not find rest amid the things of time and sense: Open to us, we pray Thee, the gates of that invisible realm in which Thou dwellest. Grant that as we abide with Thee this hour we may feel Thy greatness over our incompleteness and Thy rest round about our restlessness. Deliver us from bondage of sin and fear, and enable us, by Thy grace, to face life in this new year with the calm assurance of those whose confidence is in Thee. Hear us for Thy mercy's sake. Amen. (91 ad)

Scripture Selections (50, 157, 151, 128)

A — *I Peter*	4:12–19	You Are Partakers of Christ's Sufferings
Matt.	2:13–23	The Flight to Egypt
(Episcopalians are referred to *Matt. 2:19–23* and *Isa. 6:1–3.*)		
E — *James*	4:13–17	Commit All Affairs to God's Providence
Matt.	16:1–4	The Pharisees Require a Sign
Ps.	73:23–28	God Our Strength
P — *I John*	4:9–16	He That Abideth in Love Abideth in God
Luke	2:21–32	The Naming of Jesus. The Nunc Dimittis

T — *Acts*   *19:1–7*   The Spirit Given by the Laying On of Paul's Hands

    Mark   *6:20–29*   John the Baptist Beheaded

General Prayer

For Inward Grace

Almighty God, the unfailing Source of light and mercy, who hast brought us to the beginning of this year, and art sparing us to love Thee and to keep Thy commandments: Prepare us, we beseech Thee, for the coming days. Let Thy grace enlighten our darkness and strengthen our weakness. Inspire us with new purposes and hopes. Deepen within our hearts love of truth and goodness. Enable us to discern the solemn meaning of these earthly days, and the high and sacred purpose for which they are given. (76 ab)

Confirm Our Resolution

Everliving God, by whose mercy we have entered the gateway of another year: Grant that we may walk with humble and grateful hearts; and confirm our resolution, we beseech Thee, to walk more closely in Thy way, and labor more faithfully in Thy service, according to the teaching and example of Thy Son our Lord. (129 ab)

Prayer of Confession

O God, gracious and long-suffering, who delightest in mercy and willest that all should return unto Thee and live: Pardon, we beseech Thee, our many slack and empty hours, our distrust of Thee, our impatience, the evil we have done, the good we have left undone, and all the manifold transgressions of which our consciences are afraid, and grant us grace to live throughout the year, and the remainder of our life, in love, obedience, and devout submission to Thy will. (53 ad)

Special Intercessions
For the Nations

O Lord God of our fathers, who in Thy goodness hast led Thy people by wondrous ways and who makest the nations to praise Thee: We beseech Thee to pour Thy abundant blessing upon the nations of the world. Grant that all, of whatever race, color, or tongue, may be united in the bond of brotherhood, and in the one fellowship of faith, so that we may be found a people acceptable to Thee. (37 ad)

FOR GRACE TO FOLLOW THE PRINCE OF PEACE

O God, who by the leading of a star didst manifest Thy only Son to the Gentiles, and didst guide them to the place where He lay: Mercifully grant that we, to whom Thou hast revealed Him more clearly by the light of Thy glorious Gospel, may ever follow Him as the Prince of Peace, and be so led and governed by His Spirit, that we may be brought at last to that place where He now is, there to enjoy the perfect fulfillment of His promise of peace and blessedness. (107 ab)

FOR CONSECRATION

O God, our God and the God of our fathers: We consecrate to Thee all that we are and all that we have, the powers of our mind, the members of our body, our wealth, and our time. Grant us grace, O Father of mercies, to employ all to Thy glory, and to live in obedience to Thy commands, with an ardent and humble desire to continue Thine throughout the endless ages of eternity. Through Jesus Christ our Lord. Amen. (33)

Offertory Sentence and Prayer

In recognition of God's Lordship over all, David said, "For all things come of Thee, and of Thine own have we given Thee." *I Chron. 29:14.*

Our Father, who dost permit us to share in the task of bringing men to know and love Thee: We bring an offering with glad hearts, praying Thy blessing upon those who have given it. May it be wisely used, in Jesus' Name. Amen. (64)

9. FIRST SUNDAY AFTER THE EPIPHANY

January 7–13
Liturgical Color: White

Opening Sentences

1. I will fill this house with glory, saith the Lord of Hosts. . . .
And in this place will I give peace. *Hag. 2:7, 9.*

2. Bless ye the Lord, all ye servants of the Lord. *Ps. 134:1.*

Invocation

Almighty and everlasting God, in whom we live and move and
have our being, who hast created us for Thyself, so that our hearts
are restless till they find rest in Thee: Grant unto us purity of heart
and strength of purpose so that no selfish passion may hinder us
from knowing Thy will, and no weakness from doing it. Grant us
Thy light that we may see life clearly, and in Thy service find perfect freedom. For Thy mercy's sake. Amen. (142 ad)

Scripture Selections (50, 128)

A — *Rom.*	*12:1–5*	The Reasonable Service
Luke	*2:41–52*	The Boy Jesus in the Temple
P — *Isa.,*	*ch. 55*	Ho, Everyone That Thirsteth
Ps.	*47*	God the King of the Earth

General Prayer

SCATTER THE DARKNESS

Heavenly Father: We adore Thee as the Light in whom is no darkness at all. We thank Thee that Thou hast sent forth Thy only Son
to be the Light to shine to all that dwell in the land of the shadow
of death. Speedily scatter the darkness of heathenism and bring all
people and nations to Thee that they may live in the light of His
Gospel. To this end, Heavenly Father, strengthen Thy servants to
pray, labor, and wait for Thy everlasting Kingdom. Quicken our
faith, and make the last charge of the Master ever to ring in our

ears: Go into all the world and preach the Gospel to every creature. (66 and 140)

Saviour, Help Us

Merciful Saviour: We thank Thee that Thou didst come into the world to be about Thy Father's house to save us from sin. We praise Thee that Thou hast purchased our pardon. Conform our wills to Thine; take our hearts and fill them with Thy love; take our lips and speak through them; take our lives and use them to Thy blessed purpose; make us, O Lord, vessels of Thy grace, examples of Thy teaching, and witnesses of Thy truth and glory. (66 and 127)

For Humility

O God our Father: Since he who stands must take heed lest he fall, deliver us this day from the foolishness of pride. Grant that neither outwardly nor inwardly we boast of our imagined powers. Give us such respect for the real tasks of life that we may know that they are beyond our unaided strength; that with a clean mind and a pure heart we may turn to Thee for help by which alone we may stand unashamed when the day is done. (52 ad)

Holy Spirit, Help Us

Holy Spirit, Spirit of wisdom and of power: Help our infirmities. Enable us to run with perseverance the race that is set before us, looking to Jesus, the Pioneer and Perfecter of our faith. (66 ad)

Special Intercessions
For Those Who Suffer

Our Father: Graciously hear our intercessions for those who suffer from physical pain and those who suffer from loneliness, frustration, unkindness, or some other cause. Give them the comforting assurance that all will be well with them and theirs; grant them the grace to forget self in the daily service of others, making their difficulties less important than the promotion of kindness and good will. Teach us all anew again and again that it is in losing our lives in the service of others that we find our highest joy. (109)

For the Young

O Triune God, who out of the mouths of babes and sucklings hast ordained strength: Reveal Thyself to our children, we beseech Thee, and grant them an entrance into Thy heavenly Kingdom; that, being born again of Thy Spirit and taught by the Lord Jesus, they may grow up before Thee in purity of heart and sincerity of faith, following the example of Christ. (129 ad)

Prepare Us for Service

O God, who appointest all things to a destined and holy end, and requirest of man a reasonable service: Quicken in us, we beseech Thee, the sense of a gracious presence and power in the world, of a providence that never slumbers, of a love that never fails, and so unite us with Thyself in our aspirations and thoughts that with our whole might we may live in Thy favor. Prepare us in this hour of meditation and prayer for another week of faithful labor and generous service of our fellow men. In the Name of Jesus Christ our Lord. Amen. (53 ad)

Offertory Sentence and Prayer

"You tithe mint and dill and cummin, and have neglected the weightier matters of the law, justice and mercy and faith; these you ought to have done, without neglecting the others." *Matt. 23:23, R.S.V.*

O Lord our God, King of all the earth, who hast given us all things richly to enjoy: Accept of Thy infinite goodness the offerings of Thy people, which in obedience to Thy commandment, and in honor of Thy Name, they yield and dedicate unto Thee; and grant unto us Thy blessing, that the same being devoted to Thy service may be used for Thy glory. Through Jesus Christ our Lord. Amen. (116)

Suggestion

A full emphasis on missions may be found in unit 47.

10. SECOND SUNDAY AFTER THE EPIPHANY

January 14–20

Liturgical Color: White; *Episcopalians:* Green

Opening Sentences

1. The Lord is great, and greatly to be praised: He is to be feared above all gods. Honor and majesty are before Him: strength and beauty are in His sanctuary. *Ps. 96:4, 6.*

2. Ho, every one that thirsteth, . . . come ye, buy, and eat; yea, come, buy wine and milk without money and without price. *Isa. 55:1.*

Invocation

Almighty God, who art our Father: We lift up our hearts to Thee, invoking Thy blessing. Cleanse our hearts that we may ascend to Thy holy presence, and worship Thee in the beauty of holiness. We give Thee thanks, O Lord, for this day, and for this place of quiet, set amid our hurrying life, hallowed by memories of days gone by, and dedicated to the life of the soul and the service of faith. May it be to us a place of rest and joy, of light and revelation; so manifest Thyself to us that all that is best in us may be called forth to praise Thee, who art the health of our countenance and our God. Amen. (96 ad)

Scripture Selections (50, 157, 128)

A — *Rom.* *12:6–16a*   Love Without Dissimulation
    John   *2:1–11*   The Wedding at Cana
    (Episcopalians since 1928 are also referred to *Mark 1:1–11.*)
P — *Mark* *1:14–28*   Jesus Came Preaching the Gospel of God
    Ps.   27   The Lord Is My Light and My Salvation

General Prayer

THANKS FOR THE REVELATION

O God, our Heavenly Father: We give Thee thanks that Thou hast crowned the revelation of Thyself in Thy Son, Jesus Christ. In

Him dost Thou show Thyself to us as a loving and merciful Father. (66 ad)

For Illumination

O Lord of light: Make pure our hearts, and we shall see Thee; reveal Thyself to us, and we shall love Thee. Strengthen our wills, and we shall choose the good from the evil, and day by day manifest in the world the glory and power of Thy blessed Gospel, which Thou hast made known to us through Thy Son Jesus Christ. (46)

For the Nations

Almighty God, who art worthy to be had in reverence by all Thy children: Bestow Thy grace upon all nations of the earth. Especially do we entreat Thee to bless our land, and all its inhabitants, and all who are in authority. Cause Thy glory to dwell among us, and let Thy mercy and truth, righteousness and peace, everywhere prevail. To this end, we commend all our schools, and pray Thee to make them nurseries of useful knowledge and of Christian virtues. (57)

For Missions and Missionaries

O Lord Jesus Christ, who didst charge Thy apostles that they should preach the Gospel to every nation: Prosper, we pray Thee, all missions, both at home and abroad. Give them all things needful for their work, making them centers of spiritual life, to the quickening of many souls, and the glory of Thy holy Name. Support, guide, and bless all Thy servants who are called to labor; give them grace to witness to the faith; endow them with burning zeal and love, making them patient under all disappointments, and meekly submissive under all persecutions, that they may turn many to righteousness, and may themselves win a crown of everlasting glory. (137 ad)

Special Intercessions
For Trust

Serene Son of God, whose will subdued the troubled waters and laid to rest the fears of men: Let Thy majesty master us and Thy power of calm control us. Subdue every storm, without and within. Deepen the stillness of our inmost thoughts, and refresh us with the quiet springs of eternity. Confirm in us the knowledge of Thy presence as our companion on life's voyage, that at length our hearts may find rest in Thee. (122 ad from four short prayers)

For Dedication of Life

O God: As we look down the future years, make us sure that we place our lives where the need is greatest; deepen our love, that, giving ourselves up wholly to Thy will, we may serve Thee faithfully all the rest of our life, becoming channels of Thy infinite love. And this we ask through the inspiration of Him who sanctified and elevated all of life, even Jesus Christ our Lord. Amen. (131 ad and 89)

Offertory Sentence and Prayer

Every man according as he purposeth in his heart, so let him give; not grudgingly, or of necessity: for God loveth a cheerful giver. *II Cor.* 9:7.

Our Father in heaven: We acknowledge Thee as the Giver of every good and perfect gift. We bring Thee now a portion of that which Thou hast given us, praying that Thou wilt accept it and use it, both here and throughout the world. In Jesus' Name. Amen. (91 ad)

11. THE TRANSFIGURATION OF OUR LORD (Sixth Sunday After the Epiphany)

January 14 to February 14 (The Transfiguration is generally observed the last Sunday after the Epiphany, except when there is only one Sunday after the Epiphany)

Liturgical Color: White

For the Choir

Eternal God, who art pleased when Thy children long for Thee: Prepare us inwardly for the service we are about to render, that all may see the glory of Thy Son and listen to Him. In the Name of Him who is always pleasing to Thee. Amen. (109)

Opening Sentences

1. I was glad when they said unto me, Let us go into the house of the Lord. Our feet shall stand within thy gates, O Jerusalem. . . . To give thanks unto the Name of the Lord. *Ps. 122:1, 2, 4.*

2. Give unto the Lord the glory due unto His Name; worship the Lord in the beauty of holiness. *Ps. 29:2.*

3. God, who commanded the light to shine out of darkness, shine in your hearts, to give the light of the knowledge of the glory of God, in the face of Jesus Christ. (135)

Invocations

1. O God, who on the Mount didst reveal Thy only-begotten Son, wonderfully transfigured, in raiment white as the light: Mercifully grant that we, being delivered from the noise and confusion of this world, may be permitted to behold the King in His beauty, who with Thee, and the Holy Spirit, liveth and reigneth, one God, world without end. (126 ad)

2. Almighty God, our Heavenly Father, who hast promised to hear us when we call upon Thee in the Name of Thy Son: We beseech Thee to regard us in Thy mercy, as we are here assembled to offer unto Thee our praises and our prayers, and to hear Thy Word;

and so to raise our thoughts and desires to Thyself, that we may render to Thee an acceptable service. Through Jesus Christ our Lord. Amen. (27)

Scripture Selections (50, 151)

A —	II Peter	1:16–21	We Have a Sure Word of Prophecy
	Matt.	17:1–9	The Transfiguration of Jesus
E —	II Cor.	3:12–18	The Gospel of Life and Liberty
	John	5:39–47	Search the Scriptures
	Ex.	3:1–6	God Appears to Moses in the Burning Bush
T —	I Peter	1:3–21	Redeemed with the Precious Blood of Christ
	Luke	7:1–10	Christ Heals the Centurion's Servant
S —	II Peter	3:14–18	Exhortation to Remain Steadfast
	Mark	9:2–13	The Transfiguration of Christ
	Gen.	28:10–22	Jacob's Vision of the Ladder

General Prayer

Grant Us a Vision

O God, who in the mystery of Thy Word made flesh hast caused a new light to shine: Vouchsafe to us who long for Thy courts, we beseech Thee, a vision of Thy glory and honor, through the mediation of Thy well-beloved Son, our Lord and Saviour. (122 ad)

Shine into our hearts, O loving Master, by the pure light of the knowledge of Thyself, and open the eyes of our mind to the contemplation of Thy teaching, and put into us the fear of Thy blessed commandments; that trampling down all that is worldly, we may follow a spiritual life, thinking and doing things according to Thy good pleasure. (7 ab)

For the Indwelling of the Spirit

Spirit of purity and grace: We thank Thee for the glory of our early visions and for Thy rebukes of our low ambitions. Guide us, we pray Thee, that we may no longer fear that which is ordinary. Let our common task glow again with the light of holy purpose, and give us some part in Thy abiding work. Move us to speak and achieve the things that conform to Thy purposes, ever uniting us more closely to Jesus in whom we offer ourselves anew to Thee. (74 ad)

For Christian Education

Almighty God, our Heavenly Father, who hast committed to Thy holy Church the care and nurture of Thy children: Enlighten with Thy wisdom those who teach and those who learn, that, rejoicing in the knowledge of Thy truth, they may worship Thee and serve Thee from generation to generation. (126 ab)

An Intercession

Remember again, O Lord, those who have bidden us to pray for them in time of prayer and supplication. O Lord our God, give comfort to those who are bereaved; heal speedily those who are sick, for Thou art the Life, the Hope, and the Deliverer of us all. (1 ad)

Special Intercessions
For the Whole State of Christ's Church

Almighty and everliving God, who by Thy holy Apostle hast taught us to make prayers, and supplications, and to give thanks for all men: We humbly beseech Thee to inspire continually the Universal Church with the spirit of truth, unity, and concord. And grant that all those who confess Thy holy Name may agree in the truth of Thy holy Word, and live in unity and godly love. (126 ab)

We beseech Thee also so to direct and dispose the hearts of all Christian rulers, that they may truly and impartially administer justice, to the punishment of wickedness and vice, and to the maintenance of Thy true religion and virtue. (126)

Give grace, O Heavenly Father, to all ministers, that they may, by their teaching, set forth Thy true and lively Word, and rightly and duly administer the holy sacraments. (126 ad)

And to all Thy people give Thy heavenly grace; and especially to this congregation here present; that, with meek heart and due reverence, they may hear and receive Thy holy Word; truly serving Thee in holiness and righteousness all the days of their life. (126)

Give us grace so to follow the good examples of those who have gone before, that with them we may be partakers of Thy heavenly

Kingdom. Grant this, O Father, for Jesus Christ's sake, our only Mediator and Advocate. Amen. (126 ad)

Offertory Sentence and Prayer

Let your light so shine before men, that they may see your good works, and glorify your Father which is in heaven. *Matt. 5:16.*

We thank Thee, O Heavenly Father, for all Thy goodness unto us, for life and all its blessings. Give us loyal hearts, and grant that, as we bring our gift to Thy altar, it may be the symbol of the consecration of all that we are and all that we have to the fulfillment of Thy will. And Thine shall be the glory, now and forever. Amen. (113)

12. SEPTUAGESIMA SUNDAY

January 18 to February 21 (Nine Weeks Before Easter)
Liturgical Color: Violet; *Lutherans:* Green (Violet Recommended in 156)

Opening Sentences

And a voice came out of the throne, saying, Praise our God, all ye His servants, and ye that fear Him, both small and great. And I heard as it were the voice of a great multitude, and as the voice of many waters, and as the voice of mighty thunderings, saying, Alleluia: for the Lord God Omnipotent reigneth. Let us be glad and rejoice, and give honor to Him. *Rev. 19:5–7.*

Invocation

God of all grace: Grant us Thy peace which passes understanding, that the quietness that comes from friendliness with Thee and our fellow men may possess our souls. Withdrawn awhile from the turmoil of the world, help us to recover the strength that we have lost, and pass victoriously through all the troubles of this our earthly life. Through Jesus Christ our Lord. Amen. (59 ad)

Scripture Selections (50, 157, 151)

A — *I Cor.*   *9:24–27*   The Incorruptible Crown
  Matt.   *20:1–16*   The Laborers in the Vineyard
  (Lutherans list *I Cor. 9:24 to 10:5.*)
E — *Phil.*   *1:27 to 2:4*   Being of One Accord
  Luke   *10:38–42*   But One Thing Is Needful
  Jer.   *9:23, 24*   Cause for True Glorying

General Prayer

PREPARE US FOR A BETTER LIFE

O merciful Father, who in compassion for Thy sinful children didst send Thy Son Jesus Christ to be the Saviour of the world: Grant us grace to feel and to lament our share in the evil which made it needful for Him to suffer and to die for our salvation. Help us by self-denial, prayer, and meditation to prepare our hearts for deeper penitence and a better life. (127 ab)

Open our eyes that we may see Him; enlighten our understanding that we may know Him; and strengthen our wills that we may follow Him. Unite Thy people in fellowship through prayer. Refresh us in the inner life; purify us by Thy cleansing power; and bless us by the indwelling of Thy Holy Spirit. (38 ad)

SPECIAL INTERCESSIONS
FOR MISSIONARIES AFAR

O Thou who rulest by Thy providence over land and sea: Defend and guide and bless the messengers of Christ; in danger be their shield, in darkness their hope; enrich their word and work with wisdom, joy, and power, and let them gather souls for Thee in far fields white for the harvest. (140 ad)

O Thou, who by Thy Holy Spirit workest wonders in secret: Open the eyes that dimly look for light to see the Son of righteousness; open the minds that seek the unknown to know Thee as our Heavenly Father in Christ; open the hearts that hunger for righteousness to find eternal peace in Christ. Deliver all prisoners of ignorance and captives of idolatry; break down the bars of error, and dispel the shadows of the ancient night; lift up the gates, and let the King of Glory and the Prince of Peace come in. (140 ad)

GENERAL INTERCESSION

O God: We most heartily beseech Thee to bless all Thy people. Send down into their hearts the peace of heaven, and grant us also the peace of this life. Give life to all of us, and let no deadly sin prevail against us, or any of Thy people. Deliver all who are in trouble, for Thou art our God, who givest hope to the hopeless and help to the helpless. Give Thy pardon and refreshment to every Christian soul, whether in affliction or error, and give fervor of spirit to those who are lukewarm in their faith. (22 ad and 14 ad)

FOR A CROWN OF GLORY

Almighty God, from whose hand alone Thy people may receive the crown of glory: Grant us, in the race that is set before us, such temperance and self-discipline that, reaching forth unto newness of life, we may obtain the prize of Thy high calling which Thou hast revealed to us in Him who is the righteous Judge, our Saviour Jesus Christ. Amen. (122)

Offertory Sentence and Prayer

If the readiness is there, it is acceptable according to what a man has, not according to what he has not. *II Cor. 8:12, R.S.V.*

O God, in whose sight the sacrifice of a contrite heart is more precious than whole burnt offerings: Grant that we may, with all our earthly things, yield also unto Thee the obedience of our wills, that our sacrifice may not be in vain. Through Jesus Christ our Lord. Amen. (116 ab)

13. SEXAGESIMA SUNDAY

January 25 to February 28 (Eight Weeks Before Easter)

Liturgical Color: Violet; *Lutherans:* Green (Violet Recommended in 156)

For the Choir

All-gracious God: We thank Thee for putting music in our hearts and words of joy on our lips. Guide us in every movement that in the spirit of real reverence we may exalt Thy Name. Through Jesus Christ our Lord. Amen. (109)

Opening Sentences

1. O give thanks unto the Lord; call upon His Name: make known His deeds among the people. Sing unto Him, sing psalms unto Him: talk ye of all His wondrous works. *Ps. 105:1, 2.*

2. Cast thy burden upon the Lord, and He shall sustain thee. *Ps. 55:22.*

Invocation

Thou holy One who inhabitest eternity: Visit us with an inward vision of Thy glory, that we may bow our hearts before Thee, and obtain that grace which Thou hast promised to the lowly. Through Jesus Christ our Saviour. Amen. (129 ad)

Scripture Selections (50, 57, 151, 126)

A — *II Cor.* *11:19–31*   My Grace Is Sufficient for Thee
  Luke *8:4–15*   The Parable of the Sower
  (Lutherans list *II Cor. 11:19 to 12:9.*)
E — *Phil.* *1:12–21*   Christ Shall Be Magnified
  John *11:20–27*   I Am the Resurrection, and the Life
  Amos *8:11, 12*   A Famine of God's Word

General Prayer

THANKS FOR TENDER MERCIES

Almighty and most merciful God, the Father of our Lord Jesus Christ: We give Thee thanks for all Thy goodness and tender mercies, especially for the gift of Thy dear Son, and for the revelation of Thy will and grace; and we beseech Thee so to implant Thy Word in us, that, in good and honest hearts, we may keep it, and bring forth fruit by patient continuance in well-doing. (57)

For the Church

Most heartily we beseech Thee so to rule and govern Thy Church Universal, that it may be preserved in the pure doctrine of Thy saving Word, whereby faith toward Thee may be strengthened, and love increased in us toward all mankind. (57 ad)

Send forth Thy light and Thy truth unto the uttermost parts of the earth. Raise up faithful pastors and missionaries to preach the Gospel in our own land and to all nations; and guide, protect, and prosper them in all labors. (57)

Bless, we pray Thee, the institutions of the Church; its colleges, its seminaries, and all its schools; that they may send forth men and women to serve Thee, in the ministry of the Word, the ministry of mercy, and all the walks of life. (57)

For Our Homes

Let the light of Thy Word ever shine within our homes. Keep the children of the Church in the covenant which Thou hast made with them in holy Baptism; and grant all parents grace to bring them up in faith toward Thee and in obedience to Thy will. (57)

For All in Authority

Grant also health and prosperity to all that are in authority, especially to the President (and Congress) of the United States, the Governor (and Legislature) of this Commonwealth, and to all our judges and magistrates, and endow them with grace to rule after Thy good pleasure, to the maintenance of righteousness, and to the hindrance and punishment of wickedness, that we may lead a quiet and peaceable life, in all godliness and honesty. (57)

Comfort Those in Trouble

All who are in trouble, want, sickness, anguish of labor, peril of death, or any other adversity, especially those who are in suffering for Thy Name and for Thy truth's sake, comfort, O God, with Thy Holy Spirit, that they may receive and acknowledge their afflictions as the manifestation of Thy Fatherly will. (57)

Remember Not Our Sins

And although we have deserved Thy righteous wrath and punishment, yet we entreat Thee, O most merciful Father, remember not the sins of our youth, nor our many transgressions, but out of Thy unspeakable goodness, grace, and mercy, defend us from all harm and danger of body and soul. Preserve us from false and pernicious doctrine, from war and bloodshed, from plague and pestilence, from all calamity by fire and water, from hail and tempest, from failure of harvest and from famine, from anguish of heart and despair of Thy mercy, and from an evil death. And in every time of trouble, show Thyself a very present Help, the Saviour of all men, and especially of those who believe. (57 ad)

Remake Us

O God, our everlasting hope, who holdest us in life, and orderest our lot: Strip us of every proud thought; fill us with patient tenderness for others; make us ready to help, and quick to forgive. And then, fix every grace, compose every fear, by giving us a steady trust in Thy eternal reality, behind the changes of time and delusions of men. (88 ab)

Give Success

Cause also the needful fruits of the earth to prosper, that we may enjoy them in due season. Give success to all lawful occupations on land and sea, to all pure arts and useful knowledge; and crown them with Thy blessing. (57)

Special Intercessions
Grant These Requests

These, and whatsoever other things Thou wouldst have us ask of Thee, O God, vouchsafe unto us, for the sake of the bitter sufferings and death of Jesus Christ, Thy only Son, our Lord and Saviour, who liveth and reigneth with Thee and the Holy Spirit, ever one God, world without end. Amen. (57 ad)

Offertory Sentence and Prayer

Now concerning the contribution for the saints: . . . On the first day of every week, each of you is to put something aside and save, as he may prosper. *I Cor. 16:1, 2, R.S.V.*

Eternal and ever-blessed God, from whom all holy desires, all good counsels, and all just works proceed: Accept the offering which we now make unto Thee; and grant that our small gift may not be lost in the wide world, but that it may reappear in the blessing of many lives to which it shall minister in Thy Name. Through Jesus Christ our Lord. Amen. (116)

14. QUINQUAGESIMA SUNDAY

February 1 to March 7 (Sunday Before Lent)
Liturgical Color: Violet; *Lutherans:* Green (Violet Recommended in 156)

Opening Sentences

1. Thou shalt love the Lord thy God with all thy heart, and with all thy soul, and with all thy strength, and with all thy mind. *Luke 10:27.*

2. Thus saith the Lord, Let not the wise man glory in his wisdom, neither let the mighty man glory in his might, let not the rich man glory in his riches: but let him that glorieth glory in this, that he understandeth and knoweth Me, that I am the Lord which exercise loving-kindness, judgment, and righteousness, in the earth: for in these things I delight, saith the Lord. *Jer. 9:23, 24.*

Invocation

O Lord our God: Accept now, in Thy endless mercy, the sacrifice of our worship and thanksgiving, and grant unto us all such requests as may be wholesome for us. Remember, O Lord, according to the multitude of Thy mercies, Thy whole Church; all who join us in prayer and praise; pour out upon us the riches of Thy mercy, so that, redeemed in soul and body, we may ever praise Thy wonderful and holy Name. Through Jesus Christ our Lord. Amen. (18 ad)

Scripture Selections (50, 151)

A —	*I Cor., ch. 13*		Faith, Hope, and Love
	Luke	*18:31-43*	Jesus Foretells His Passion
E —	*I Cor.*	*1:21-31*	We Preach Christ Crucified
	Mark	*10:35-45*	The Son of Man Came to Minister
	Jer.	*8:4-9*	The Impenitence of God's People
T —	*Mark*	*8:27-38*	Christ Foretells His Suffering
	Jer.	*8:19-22*	Is There No Balm in Gilead?

General Prayer

THANKS FOR LIFE

O God of Love: We thank Thee for life and love, for the mystery and majesty of existence, for the world of beauty which surrounds us, for everything Thou hast given us richly to enjoy; for health and vigor, for the love and care of home, for joys of friendship, and for every loving gift. (97 and 136)

THANKS FOR THE TIES THAT BIND

We thank Thee for the glimpses of nobility in human life which redeem it from sordidness and reassure us that Thy image is in the heart of man. We are grateful for the ties that bind us to our fellow men; for our common toil in industry and marts of trade; for our joint inheritance as citizens of this nation; for traditions and customs hallowed by age through which our passions are ordered and channeled; for the love of beauty, truth, and goodness by which we rise above the chasms of race and nation; for the faith of our fathers by which we claim kinship with the past and gain strength for the present; for the love of dear ones in our homes and for the enlarging responsibilities and sobering duties of our family life; for the serenity of old people who redeem us from fretfulness and for the faith and courage of youth who save us from sloth. (97 ad)

FORGIVE WHAT WE HAVE BEEN

Our Heavenly Father, who by Thy love hast made us, and through Thy love hast kept us, and in Thy love wouldst make us perfect: We humbly confess that we have not loved Thee with all our heart and soul and mind and strength, and that we have not loved one another as Christ hath loved us. Forgive us for what we have been; help us to amend what we are; and in Thy Spirit direct what we shall be. (48 ad)

FOR LOVE TO EACH OTHER

O Lord our God, who hast taught us in Thy Word to love one another: Give us grace, we pray Thee, to fulfill this law of Christ.

Instill in our hearts the spirit of charity. Make us centers of radiant good will. Preserve us from harsh judgment. Help us to judge others as we would be judged, to serve as we would be served, to understand as we would be understood. Teach us to be kind one toward another, tenderhearted, generous to each other as Thou hast been generous to us in Christ. (72)

GLORIFY THE CROSS

As disciples of the Man of Sorrows, help us steadfastly to set our faces to go to our Jerusalem, prepared to be obedient unto death, seeking only for strength to glorify the cross Thou layest on us. (76 ad)

SPECIAL INTERCESSIONS
FOR SUFFERERS

God of all comfort: We commend to Thy mercy all those upon whom any cross or tribulation is laid; the nations that are afflicted with famine, pestilence, or war; those of our brethren who suffer persecution for the sake of the Gospel; all such as are in danger by sea or land; and all persons oppressed with poverty, sickness, or any infirmity of body or sorrow of mind. We pray particularly for the sick and afflicted members of this church (and for any such known only to ourselves, whom we name in our hearts before Thee). May it please Thee to show them Thy Fatherly kindness in the midst of affliction, that their hearts may turn to Thee, and receive perfect consolation, healing, and deliverance from their troubles. (4 ab)

FOR MORE LOVE TO GOD

O Lord God: Accept our humble thanks for Thy great mercy bestowed upon us. We confess that we are not worthy of the least of all Thy mercies; yet grant, we beseech Thee, that every fresh proof of Thy goodness may cause us to love Thee more and more, and make us to use our strength and all Thy gifts in doing Thy holy will more perfectly for the time to come. Through Jesus Christ our Lord. Amen. (13)

Offertory Sentence and Prayer

Let us not love in word or speech but in deed and in truth. *I John 3:18, R.S.V.*

O God, the Fountain of all good: We bring to Thee our gifts, according as Thou hast prospered us. Enable us, with our earthly things, to give Thee the love of our hearts and the service of our lives. Let Thy favor, which is life, and Thy loving-kindness, which is better than life, be upon us now and always. Through Jesus Christ our Lord. Amen. (116 as ad in 46)

15. ASH WEDNESDAY (First Lenten Service)
February 4 to March 11 (46 Days Before Easter)
Color: Violet

For the Choir

O God of Love, who didst bid us to come before Thy presence with singing and into Thy courts with praise: Give us reverent spirits and joyful hearts that we may magnify Thy Name in spirit and truth. For Jesus' sake. Amen. (109)

Opening Sentences

1. They that wait upon the Lord shall renew their strength; they shall mount up with wings as eagles; they shall run, and not be weary; and they shall walk, and not faint. *Isa. 40:31.*

2. If we say that we have no sin, we deceive ourselves, and the truth is not in us. If we confess our sins, He is faithful and just to forgive us our sins, and to cleanse us from all unrighteousness. *I John 1:8, 9.*

Invocation

O God, who makest Thyself known in the stillness: Help us to feel Thy presence in this sacred house set apart from the busy world; grant us grace to worship Thee in spirit and truth to the comfort of our souls and the upbuilding of every good purpose and holy desire. May we worship Thee not with our lips only at this hour, but in word and deed all the days of our lives. Through Jesus Christ our Lord. Amen. (119 and 131)

Scripture Selections (50, 57, 132)

A —	*Joel*	*2:12–19*	Turning to God and Fasting
	Matt.	*6:16–21*	Fasting and Laying Up Treasures in Heaven
O —	*Isa.*	*59:12–21*	The Spiritual Armor
	I John	*1:5–10*	The Blood Cleanses
	Luke	*6:20–49*	The Sermon on the Mount
	Ps. 6; 32; 38; 51; 102; 130; 143		Penitential Psalms

General Prayer
FOR AN EVENING IN LENT
O God, the Fountain of Life and the Sun of our souls: (42)

Thanks be unto Thee for permitting us again to observe the sacred season of Lent. Accept our gratitude for Thy love, which was so great that Thou didst send Thy only Son, that whoever believes in Him should not perish but have eternal life. (66 ad)

Forbid, O God, that we should forget, amid our earthly comforts, the pains and mortal anguish that our Lord endured for our salvation. Grant us a true vision of all that He suffered, in His betrayal, His lonely agony, His false trial, His mocking and scourging, and the torture of death upon the cross. (127)

FOR DISCIPLINE
We beseech Thee, most gracious God, to preserve us from the cares of this life, lest we become too much entangled in them; also from the many necessities of the body, lest we should be ensnared by pleasure; and from whatever is an obstacle to the soul, lest we should be overthrown. Give us strength to resist, patience to endure, and constancy to persevere. (15 ad)

FOR SOCIAL JUSTICE
Almighty God, who hast created man in Thy own image: Grant us grace fearlessly to contend against evil, and to make no peace with oppression; and that we may reverently use our freedom, help us to employ it in the maintenance of justice among men and nations, to the glory of Thy holy Name. (126 ab)

SPECIAL INTERCESSIONS
FOR THOSE IN SORROW, IN MENTAL DARKNESS
God of infinite compassion, God of all comfort: Reveal Thyself as the Light of Life to those who have been brought into the darkness of sorrow. Strengthen the hearts that faint under a heavy burden. Let them know that in their distress Thou dost care for them with unfailing tenderness. Help them to bear their affliction with patience. (44 ad)

Have mercy upon those living in mental darkness. Restore them to strength of mind and cheerfulness of spirit, and give them health and peace. (48 ab)

For Gratitude and Patience Among the Sick

O God, enable those who are experiencing Thy healing powers to have a true spirit of gratitude, that they may love to thank Thee for all Thy benefits. Help those who are awaiting Thy grace to be patient rather than anxious; restful instead of overly conscious of worrying cares; and cheerful for the angels of mercy who bring help for healing. (139 ad)

For all Thy mercies we thank Thee in the Name of Him who suffered for us all. Amen. (139 ad)

Offertory Sentence and Prayer

"If any man would come after Me, let him deny himself and take up his cross and follow Me." *Matt. 16:24, R.S.V.*

O God, who lovest those who hear Thy Word and keep it in faithful hearts: Be pleased to bless this offering for the spreading of Thy saving message among Thy people. Grant that an ever-increasing number may hear Thy Word and keep it. In the Name of Him who sustains us all. Amen. (109)

Alternate Benediction for the Lenten Season

And the peace of God, which passes all understanding, will keep your hearts and minds through Christ Jesus. *Phil. 4:7, R.S.V.* Amen.

Hymns for the Lenten Season

"Again, O Lord and Saviour"
"Ah, Dearest Jesus, How Hast Thou Offended"
"Alas! and Did My Saviour Bleed"
"Behold the Lamb of God!"
"Beneath the Cross of Jesus"
"Cross of Jesus, Cross of Sorrow"
"Forty Days and Forty Nights"
"Go to Dark Gethsemane"
"In the Cross of Christ I Glory"
"In the Hour of Trial"
"'It Is Finished,' All the Pain"
"Jesus, Refuge of the Weary"
"King of My Soul, a Crown of Thorns"
"'Lord, When Thy Kingdom Comes,' Remember Me!"

" Lord, Who Throughout These
  Forty Days "
" Man of Sorrows, Now My Soul
  Shall Greet Thee "
" My Faith Looks Up to Thee "
" Near the Cross Her Vigil
  Keeping "
" Now All Is Still "
" O Come and Mourn with Me
  Awhile "
" O Jesus, We Adore Thee "
" O Lamb of God, Still Keep
  Me "

" O Sacred Head, Now
  Wounded "
" Our Sins, Our Sorrows, Lord,
  Were Laid on Thee "
" There Is a Green Hill Far
  Away "
" ' 'Tis Finished! ' So the Saviour
  Cried "
" 'Tis Midnight; and on Olive's
  Brow "
" When I Survey the Wondrous
  Cross "

16. FIRST SUNDAY IN LENT (Invocavit)
February 8 to March 14
Color: Violet

Opening Sentences

1. Humble yourselves therefore under the mighty hand of God, that He may exalt you in due time: Casting all your care upon Him; for He careth for you. *I Peter 5:6, 7.*

2. I will cry unto God Most High; unto God that performeth all things for me. . . . Yea, in the shadow of Thy wings will I make my refuge, until these calamities be overpast. *Ps. 57:2 and 1.*

Invocation

O God, who art the Father of all the sons of men: We ask Thy blessing upon all who gather throughout the world this day to praise Thy Name, beseeching Thee to unite our worship with theirs, and so cleanse our thoughts and purify our hearts that we may offer to Thee a service acceptable in Thy sight. In the Name of our Lord, Jesus Christ. Amen. (89)

Scripture Selections (50, 151, 128)

A —	*II Cor.*	*6:1–10*	In All Things as the Ministers of God
	Matt.	*4:1–11*	The Temptation of Jesus
E —	*Heb.*	*4:15, 16*	We Have a Great High Priest
	Matt.	*16:21–26*	Losing and Finding Life
	Gen.	*22:1–14*	Abraham Offers Isaac
P —	*I John*	*2:7–17*	Love Not the World
	Luke	*4:1–13*	The Temptations of Jesus
	Isa.,	*ch. 58*	Declare Unto My People Their Transgressions
T —	*Matt.*	*11:20–24*	Christ Denounces the Cities
	Jer.	*2:17–19*	Backsliding of Israel Rebuked
	Jer.	*3:22, 23*	Backsliding Israel Invited to Return

General Prayer

THANKSGIVING FOR JESUS CHRIST

O God, whose glory is great in all the Churches, and the praise of whose Name resounds in the assemblies of Thy saints: We, Thy servants, humble ourselves before Thee; we worship Thy infinite majesty; we celebrate Thy wisdom, power, and goodness, which shine forth in the works of creation and redemption, through our Lord Jesus Christ. We bless Thee for all temporal and spiritual good which we continually receive at Thy bountiful hands; but more especially, with all Thy people assembled this day, we praise Thee that Thou didst send into the world Thy Son to save us. (27 ad)

FOR A GREATER LOVE AND OBEDIENCE

Eternal God, who art worthy of a greater love than we can either give or understand: Help us in this sacred season, by granting us grace and knowledge, to love Thee more and more. (67 ad)

Put into our hearts a continual desire to obey Thy will, and give us grace and power to fulfill the same. (39 ad)

FOR POWER OVER TEMPTATIONS

O Lord Jesus Christ, who didst conquer all temptations: Give us grace to call upon Thee as our only strength. Grant that standing in Thy strength against the powers of darkness, we may so win the victory over all evil suggestions that with singleness of heart we may serve Thee and Thee alone and prevail in our struggles against sin. (122 and 66)

ENABLE US TO PLEASE THEE

O God, who knowest the weakness and corruption of our nature, and the many temptations we meet: We humbly beseech Thee to have compassion on our infirmities, and to give us the constant assistance of Thy Holy Spirit, that we may be restrained from sin and aroused to our duty. Imprint in our hearts such a dread of Thy judgments, and such a grateful sense of Thy goodness to us, that we shall be both afraid and ashamed to offend Thee. And above all, keep our minds directed to that day when we must give a strict account of our thoughts, words, and actions. (126 ad)

For the Absent

O God, whose Fatherly care reaches to the uttermost parts of the earth: Graciously behold and bless those whom we love, now absent from us. Defend them from all dangers of soul and body (so far as that be in accordance with Thy will), and grant that both they and we, drawing nearer to Thee, may be bound together by Thy love in the communion of Thy Holy Spirit and in the fellowship of Thy saints. (126 ab)

For Those Who Suffer

O almighty and merciful Father, who art the help of the helpless: Look down with Thy mercy on all who are oppressed in mind, body, or estate; comfort and relieve them, according to their several necessities; give them patience under their suffering, and a happy issue out of all their afflictions. (58 ad)

Special Intercessions
Teach Us to Serve

Teach us, good Lord, to serve Thee as Thou deservest; to give and not to count the cost; to fight and not to heed the wounds; to labor and not to ask for ease. (23 ad)

For the Crown of Life

Finally, help us to obtain the crown of life which Thou hast promised to those who love Thee, permitting us to dwell with Thee in the mansions of the righteous forever. Amen. (67 ad)

Offertory Sentence and Prayer

"The Son of Man came to seek and to save that which was lost." *Luke 19:10, R.S.V.*

O Lord our God, the Giver of all good: We beseech Thee to behold in these our gifts the symbol of our consecration to Thy service; and grant that now and at all times our gratitude to Thee may be as great as our need of Thy mercy. Through Jesus Christ our Lord. Amen. (46 ad)

17. SECOND LENTEN SERVICE
Color: Violet

Opening Sentence

Come now, and let us reason together, saith the Lord: though your sins be as scarlet, they shall be as white as snow; though they be red like crimson, they shall be as wool. *Isa. 1:18.*

Invocation

O Lord, who art the Author of both day and night: Cover our sins with Thy mercy as Thou dost cover the earth with darkness; and grant that the Sun of Righteousness may ever shine in our hearts, to chase away the darkness of evil thoughts. Through Jesus Christ our Lord. Amen. (45)

General Prayer

CONFESSION

O God, who hast given us light, and who grievest because we have so often loved the darkness better: Thou knowest how, hour after hour, day after day, we have yielded to the temptations in our path, have done that which Thou hast forbidden, and have left undone the work Thou hast given us to do. O Thou whose voice of warning and love we have so little heeded: Call us yet again, we beseech Thee; call us that we may answer and do Thy bidding, that we may go astray from Thee no more; but that, being comforted by Thy love and upheld by Thy strength, we may fulfill our days upon earth, forgiven and at peace with Thee. (78 ab)

FOR SPIRITUAL BLESSINGS

Most High God, our loving Father, infinite in majesty: We humbly beseech Thee for all Thy servants everywhere, that Thou wouldst give us a pure mind, perfect love, purity in heart, sincerity in conduct, strength in action, and courage in distress. (8 ad)

For Humility

O Lord, who resistest the proud, and givest grace to the humble: Grant to us that true humility which was exemplified by Thyself on earth, that by our foolish pride we may never provoke Thy indignation, but receive the gifts of Thy grace in lowliness. (129 ad)

For Our Land

O God, who art the Hope of all the ends of the earth: Remember Thy whole creation and protect our land from whatever threatens its welfare, so that religion and virtue may flourish more and more. Give the spirit of wisdom and godly fear to Thy servant, the President of the United States, and to all in authority over us. Give humility to the rich and grace to use their riches to Thy glory; bless the people in their callings and families, and be Thou a refuge to the poor in their distress. Make every home a shelter from temptation and a nursery of noble youth; take also the homeless beneath Thy protection. (129 ad)

Special Intercessions
For Refuge

Lord of storm and calm, of day and night, of life and death: Grant to us faithful hearts directed to Thee and Thy unchanging love, that we may walk in lowliness toward Thee, in loving-kindness toward one another, and remain faithful through all storms and troubles of this mortal life. And unto Thee we shall offer praises forever. Amen. (139 ad)

Offertory Sentence and Prayer

"One must help the weak, remembering the words of the Lord Jesus, how He said, 'It is more blessed to give than to receive.'" *Acts 20:35, R.S.V.*

Almighty God, to whom all things belong, but who art willing to accept from us even those mercies which Thou Thyself hast bestowed: Accept these our offerings, and consecrate them that Thy Name may be glorified. This we humbly beg through our Lord and Saviour, Jesus Christ. Amen. (113 ad)

18. SECOND SUNDAY IN LENT (Reminiscere)
February 15 to March 21
Color: Violet

Opening Sentence
For thus saith the high and lofty One that inhabiteth eternity, whose Name is Holy; I dwell in the high and holy place, with him also that is of a contrite and humble spirit, to revive the spirit of the humble, and to revive the heart of the contrite ones. *Isa. 57:15.*

Invocation
O Lord our God, who hast promised that in all places where Thou dost record Thy Name Thou wilt meet Thy people to bless them: Behold us as we eagerly and penitently come before Thee, and bless us.

O eternal Goodness: Deliver us from evil. O eternal Light: Shine into our hearts. O eternal Power: Be Thou our support. Help us to seek Thy face with all our hearts. Through Jesus Christ our Lord. Amen. (70 ad)

Scripture Selections (50, 157, 151)

A —	*I Thess.*	*4:1–7*	The Will of God, Even Your Sanctification
	Matt.	*15:21–28*	The Canaanitish Woman
	(Episcopalians list *I Thess. 4:1–8.*)		
E —	*I John*	*2:12–17*	Love Not the World
	Luke	*10:17–20*	Are Your Names Written in Heaven?
	Ex.	*33:17–23*	Moses Seeks to See God's Glory
T —	*Heb.*	*2:10–15*	The Captain of Our Salvation
	Heb.	*8:8–12*	The Promise of a New Covenant
	John	*8:21–30*	Christ Predicts His Crucifixion
	Ex.	*14:13–21*	The Pursuing Egyptians Destroyed
	Isa.	*52:7–17*	Tidings of the Gospel

General Prayer

THANKS FOR JESUS CHRIST

O God, who art the hope for all the ends of the earth: We thank Thee that in loving-kindness Thou didst have mercy on us in our sins and didst not spare Thy only Son, delivering Him up for us all, that we might have everlasting life. (63 and 66)

CAST OUT OUR SIN

O God, the Father of our Lord and Saviour Jesus Christ, whose Name is great, whose goodness is inexhaustible, before whom stand thousands of thousands, and ten thousand times ten thousands, the hosts of holy angels and archangels: Touch our hearts and cast out of us every evil thought, every base desire, all envy and pride and hypocrisy, all falsehood, all deceit, all worldly anxiety, all anger, all remembrance of injuries, every motion of the flesh and spirit that is contrary to Thy holy will. (21 ad)

DELIVER US

O God, whose grace is sufficient for all our needs: Deliver us from the domination of discouragement and disappointment, fears and frustrations, selfishness and sorrow. Cause us to focus our attention on Thy Son, the Conqueror, and give us the victory which overcomes the world. (109)

FOR DOCTORS AND NURSES

O God of compassion: Bless the physicians and nurses who care for the sick and afflicted. Give faithfulness and skill to their work, efficiency to the means they employ, and help them to realize that in their best service they are serving Thee. (48)

FOR ALL POOR, HOMELESS, AND NEGLECTED FOLK

O God, almighty and merciful, who healest those who are broken in heart, and turnest the sadness of the sorrowful to joy: Let Thy Fatherly goodness be upon all that Thou hast made. Remember in Thy mercy such as are this day destitute, homeless, or forgotten of their fellow men. Uplift those who are cast down. Cheer with hope all discouraged and unhappy people. Though they be troubled on every side, suffer them not to be distressed; though they be perplexed, save them from despair. Grant this, O Lord, for the love of Him who for our sakes became poor. (126 ad)

Special Intercessions
Increase Our Zeal

Increase, O God, the faith and zeal of all Thy people, that they may more earnestly desire, and more diligently seek, the salvation of their fellow men, through the message of Thy love in Jesus Christ our Lord. Send forth a mighty call unto Thy servants to labor in the Gospel, granting unto them a heart of love, sincerity of speech, and the power of the Holy Spirit, that they may be able to persuade men to forsake sin and return unto Thee. And so bless and favor the work in this and every church that multitudes may be brought from the kingdom of evil into the Kingdom of Thy dear Son. (131 ad)

For the Right Use of Fleeting Days

O God: Since we know not what a day may bring forth, but only that the hour for serving Thee is always present, consecrate with Thy presence the way our feet may go. Lift us into the realm of faith and hope and charity, that we may be modest in our success, patient amidst disappointment, and calm in death. At the end of our days receive us into the mansions prepared and opened for us by the grace of Jesus Christ our Lord. Amen. (130 and 66)

Offertory Sentence and Prayer

" If any man would come after Me, let him deny himself and take up his cross and follow Me." *Mark 8:34, R.S.V.*

Lord of power and might, who art the Giver of all good things: We thank Thee for inscribing in our hearts the love of Thy Name and nourishing in us the growth of Thy goodness. Accept these tokens of our love for all Thy mercies. Amen. (9 ad)

19. THIRD LENTEN SERVICE
Color: Violet

For the Choir

O God of all grace: Let Thy blessing rest upon the preparation our choir members have made, that they may now fulfill their function in this sacred service. In the Name of Him who loveth us and inspireth us to love one another. Amen. (109)

Opening Sentence

For thus saith the Lord God, the Holy One of Israel; In returning and rest shall ye be saved; in quietness and in confidence shall be your strength. *Isa. 30:15.*

Invocation

Lord of the evening hour, who hast often met us at the close of day: Be our Refuge now from the noise of the world and the care of our own spirits. Grant us Thy peace. Let not the darkness of our ignorance and the folly of our sorrow and sin hide Thee from us. Draw near to us that we may be near to Thee. Speak to each of us the word that we need, and let Thy Word abide in us till it has wrought in us Thy holy will. Quicken and refresh our hearts, renew and increase our strength, so that by our worship at this time we may be enabled to serve Thee in our daily life in the spirit of Jesus Christ our Lord. Amen. (76 ad)

General Prayer

THANKSGIVING

Glory be to Thee, O God, for all Thy goodness to us and to all men. For the world in which Thou hast placed us, with all its wonder and beauty; for life and health, for food and clothing; for friends and homes; for Thy care that guards us always, and Thy faithfulness that never fails; most of all for Jesus Christ Thy only Son our Saviour, who came into this world and died for us upon the cross, and who hath revealed to us the love that passes knowledge, we thank and praise Thee, O God. (128 ad)

Bless This Hour

O God, the Fountain of Life and the Sun of our souls: Enlighten our minds and direct our hearts, that in our desires we may conform to Thy holy will, and in our prayers may seek those things Thou lovest to bestow. (42)

Grant to us the peace that the world cannot give. Deliver us from the vain things that have power over us, that no unhallowed thoughts or cares may disturb the quiet of this (evening) hour. Help us to learn wisdom, gain hope, and feel the influence of things unseen, until we rest in Thee. (127 ad)

General Supplication

Almighty God, who seest that we have no power of ourselves to help ourselves: Keep us both outwardly in our bodies and inwardly in our souls, that we may be defended from all adversities that may happen to our body, and from all evil thoughts that may assault and hurt the soul. (128 ab)

For Deliverance from Fear

Heavenly Father: Preserve us from all worldly anxieties, and grant that no clouds of this mortal life may hide us from Thy light; help us always to trust in Thy goodness in the assurance that Thou carest for us. (51 ad and 112)

For Others

O God, who never sleepest and art never weary: Give Thy angels charge over those who sleep. Have mercy upon the sick that they may obtain sleep and relaxation, allowing the healing powers of nature to do their best; on the fainthearted, that they may have hope and courage; on the lighthearted lest they forget Thee; on the dying, that they may find peace. (133 and 3)

For Those Bearing a Cross

We beseech Thee for all those who are called to bear any cross or tribulation, that it may please Thee to sustain them with the comfort of Thy Holy Spirit, until Thou shalt send a full deliverance out of all their troubles; so that through their patience and constancy Thy Kingdom may increase and shine through all the world. (125 ad)

Special Intercessions
For Brotherhood

O God, our Ruler: Give to every nation a deeper sense of brotherhood, a new respect for man and reverence for woman, a spirit of loyalty to Thy law, that all the world may reflect the radiance of Thy throne which is eternal in the heavens. For Christ's sake we pray. Amen. (37 ad)

Offertory Sentence and Prayer

Well done, good and faithful servant; thou hast been faithful over a few things, I will make thee ruler over many things: enter thou into the joy of thy lord. *Matt. 25:23.*

O Thou who hast given Thy only Son to give His very life that we might live: Help us to give as He gave, that the offering of our money may be the symbol of our life upon Thy altar. Impart the joy of Christ in our hearts as we present this offering for consecration. Hear us, we pray, for Jesus' sake. Amen. (159 ad)

20. THIRD SUNDAY IN LENT (Oculi)

February 22 to March 28
Color: Violet

For the Choir

O Thou who touchest earth, in those who reveal Thy unseen beauty: We thank Thee for all who show a musical interest. Speak peace and courage to our congregation. Grant that praising Thee we may all love Thee, and that loving Thee we may serve Thee evermore in the glad company of the followers of Jesus Christ. Amen. (99 ad)

Opening Sentences

Serve the Lord with gladness: come before His presence with singing. Enter into His gates with thanksgiving, and into His courts with praise: be thankful unto Him, and bless His Name. For the Lord is good; His mercy is everlasting; and His truth endureth to all generations. *Ps. 100:2, 4, 5.*

Invocation and Confession

Eternal God, in whom we live and move and have our being; whose face is hidden from us by our sins; and whose mercy we forget in the blindness of our hearts: Cleanse us, we beseech Thee, from all our offenses, and deliver us from proud thoughts and vain desires, that with lowliness and meekness we may draw near to Thee, confessing our faults, confiding in Thy grace, and finding in Thee our Refuge and our Strength. Through Jesus Christ Thy Son. Amen. (128)

Scripture Selections (50, 57, 157, 151)

A — *Eph.*   5:1–9   Christ Has Given Himself for Us
     Luke   11:14–26   Jesus Casting Out a Demon
     (Lutherans end the Gospel with *v. 28.*)
     (Episcopalians: *Eph. 5:1–14.*)

E — *1 Peter*	*1:13-16*	Be Ye Holy, for I Am Holy
Luke	*9:51-56*	Jesus Sets His Face to Go to Jerusalem
Jer.	*26:1-15*	Jeremiah Exhorts to Repentance
T — *Heb.*	*5:7-10*	A High Priest After the Order of Melchizedek
John	*10:24-33*	The Jews Attempt to Stone Jesus
Gen.	*22:1-19*	Abraham Offers His Son Isaac

General Prayer

A Confession

Most righteous God, who lookest down upon the children of men, and findest that there is none that is good, not one: We implore Thy mercy, that we may be wholly converted to a life filled by Thy Spirit. (66 ad)

Thanks for Love and Mercy

We thank Thee, O gracious Saviour, Thou Lamb of God who takest away the sin of the world, for Thy love and mercy expressed in all Thy words and deeds, Thy life and death. With countless multitudes we extol Thy Name, in which alone we find salvation. We do not ask that Thou wouldst safely keep us, but that Thou wilt keep us loyal to Thee, who didst face death unafraid, and dost live and reign forever. (66 and 133)

Sympathy

O God: Incline us, with the simplicity of the disciples sitting at Jesus' feet, to that good part which shall not be taken from us. Fill us with forbearance to the weak, lest we also be tempted; with pity for the suffering, seeing that we too dwell in houses of clay; with courage against temptation, knowing Thou art on our side; with a spirit of praise and love amid our joys; and with a hope befitting those whose most blessed life is hid with Christ in Thee. (88 ad)

Make Us Faithful Witnesses

O Jesus Christ, who art greater than the greatest of the sons of men; before whom we bow in reverence and adoration; whom we call Lord and Saviour and Master and Redeemer: Make us Thy faithful witnesses, to carry Thy Gospel to those who know Thee not; to speak Thy truth to those who have not heard it, or who have forgotten it; to testify by word and act that Thou art indeed the Son of the living God. (77)

Special Intercessions
For Others

O God, whose mercies never fail: We commend to Thee all who have a place in our hearts and sympathies; all who are joined to us by sacred ties; all little children who are dear to us; all our neighbors and friends; all who help us to live a faithful life. Ever pour upon them Thy blessings. For all Thy blessings we give Thee our hearty praise and thanks forever. Amen. (76 ad)

Offertory Sentence and Prayer

See that none of you repays evil for evil, but always seek to do good to one another and to all. *I Thess. 5:15, R.S.V.*

Almighty God, our Heavenly Father, who hast spared not Thy only Son, but delivered Him up for us all, and who with Him hast freely given us all things: Help us, we beseech Thee, with all our gifts to yield ourselves unto Thee, that with body, soul, and spirit we may truly serve Thee, and in Thy service find our deepest joy. Through Jesus Christ our Lord. Amen. (116)

21. FOURTH LENTEN SERVICE

Liturgical Color: Violet

A Collect for the Choir

O God of beauty, through whom there is perfect harmony: So inspire us that our hearts may be in tune with Thy goodness and our service a reflection of Thy glory. Through Jesus Christ our Lord. Amen. (109)

Opening Sentence

Seek ye the Lord while He may be found, call ye upon Him while He is near: let the wicked forsake his way, and the unrighteous man his thoughts: and let him return unto the Lord, and He will have mercy upon him; and to our God, for He will abundantly pardon. *Isa. 55:6, 7.*

Invocation

O Lord God, almighty and most merciful, whom the heaven of heavens cannot contain, much less the temples built with hands, but who also dwellest with men, and delightest to meet with people who have gathered together in the Name of Thy Son: Cleanse our hearts, we beseech Thee, from all evil thought and desire, and vouchsafe Thy Divine presence and blessing, that we may please Thee in this hour of worship and at length also obtain Thy favor with life everlasting in Thy heavenly Kingdom. Through Jesus Christ our Lord. Amen. (128 ad)

General Prayer

PRAISE FOR CHRIST'S SACRIFICE

Lord God, our Heavenly Father: We humbly worship Thee, for Thou hast made Him who knew no sin to be sin for us that we might be made righteous in Him. Praise and thanksgiving be given to Thee, Lord Jesus our Saviour, who didst love us even in the death on the cross. We glorify Thee for having redeemed us with Thy precious blood. We bless Thee, O Christ, Thou only Mediator between God and man, for all Thou didst endure for us; for every burden Thou didst bear; for every battle Thou didst fight; for every tear Thou didst shed; for every agony Thou didst suffer; for every word of consolation Thou didst utter; for bearing our griefs and carrying our sorrows. We give Thee glory, everlasting glory, for the victory which Thou didst gain. (66 ad)

CONFESSION OF SINS

Almighty God, Spirit of purity and grace, whose salvation is never far away from the contrite heart: Hear our confession of sin and have mercy upon us. For the counsels of Thy Word which have spoken vainly to us; for the pleadings of Thy Spirit to which we have not hearkened; for all forgotten vows; for the weakness of our better purposes; for our readiness to blame, and our want of thoughtfulness, patience, kindness, and sympathy; for all the good things we have wasted; and for the opportunities we have neglected, have mercy upon us, O God. (76 ad)

SPECIAL INTERCESSIONS
FOR MINISTERS

O God of all comfort, the Father of all tender mercies: We bless Thy Name for all leaders of Thy Church. We commend especially to Thy care all faithful pastors who have reached the eventide of life. We thank Thee for the godly influences which have molded their early years, for their dedication to Thy service in the Church, for the high visions of their calling, for their years of preparation and lifelong habits of study, and for their faithfulness in ministering to the needs of their congregations. Accept our hearty thanks for their work of love, and remember them and their loved ones in Thy mercy. (56 ad)

O Lord of the harvest: Raise up among the young today ministers of like devotion to Thy Church, as self-emptied and self-spending, as broad in sympathy, as courteous and kindly in spirit, as stalwart in faith, and as industrious in their work as the great ambassadors of Thy will through the ages. (56 ad)

For the Sick

O God, who dost hear all those who look to Thee for help and strength: (109) Let Thy compassion comfort those laid aside by sickness. Renew their courage. Revive their strength. Give them patience and good cheer. And lay Thy hand of healing upon their wounded souls, that inner peace may be their portion. (72)

For Grace to Die

O God, who holdest our souls in life, and hast appointed all men to die: Grant that when our earthly sojourn is ended we may neither be troubled nor dismayed; but being satisfied with Thy goodness and mercy, we may commend our spirits to Thy care; and firmly trusting in the merits of Thy Son, our Saviour, may we obtain a peaceful death and a happy entrance into glory. And this we beg for the sake of Him who died for us that we might live with Thee forever. Amen. (129 ad)

Offertory Sentences and Prayer

1. And whosoever doth not bear his cross, and come after Me, cannot be My disciple. *Luke 14:27.*

2. Paul wrote to Titus, " And let our people learn to apply themselves to good deeds, so as to help cases of urgent need, and not to be unfruitful." *Titus 3:14, R.S.V.*

O God, who by the example of Thy dear Son hast warned us that we should work while it is day, before the night comes when no man can work: Accept these symbols of our work for the task and privilege of bringing mankind to Thee. Bestow Thy favor upon the task Thou wouldst have us do. For the sake of Jesus Christ, in whose Name we pray. Amen. (127 ad)

22. FOURTH SUNDAY IN LENT (Laetare)

February 29 to April 4
Color: Violet

For the Choir

O Father in heaven, who dost give peace to Thy children through our Lord Jesus Christ: Gather up all good thoughts, holy feelings, and right intentions, that with all our hearts we may join in the joyful singing of praises for all Thy deeds of strength and mercy. To this end bless our worship. For Jesus' sake. Amen. (109)

Opening Sentence

Wherefore, seeing we also are compassed about with so great a cloud of witnesses, let us lay aside every weight, and the sin which doth so easily beset us, and let us run with patience the race that is set before us, looking unto Jesus the Author and Finisher of our faith; who for the joy that was set before Him endured the cross, despising the shame, and is set down at the right hand of the throne of God. *Heb. 12:1, 2.*

Invocation

O Thou in whom we live and have our being, who revealest Thyself on every side, and in all places of Thy vast dominion: Grant to us, who now seek Thy blessing in this worship service, help from above and an open mind within, that our thoughts and feelings may be full of reverence and love for Thee. Amen. (28 ad)

Scripture Selections (50, 57, 157, 151)

A — *Rom.*   *5:1–11*   Justified by Faith We Have Peace with God
John   *6:1–15*   The Feeding of the Five Thousand
(Lutherans: *Gal. 4:21–31* for the Epistle.)
(Episcopalians: *Gal. 4:21–31* and *John 6:1–14.*)

E — II Cor.	7:4–10	Repentance Unto Salvation
John	6:47–57	I Am the Bread of Life
Isa.	52:7–10	Tidings of the Gospel
T — Heb.	10:1–14	The Law a Shadow of Good Things to Come
John	11:47–57	The Prophecy of Caiaphas
Isa.	42:1–8	The Office of the Saviour

General Prayer

PRAISE FOR SENDING JESUS

Almighty and everlasting God, who art worthy of a greater praise than our lips can offer, and a greater love than we can give or understand: Accept our thanks for sending Thy Son to suffer death upon the cross. (126 ad)

A CONFESSION

Look understandingly upon us in our finiteness and mercifully upon our sinfulness. From lack of reverence for truth and beauty; from prejudice; from being contented with the mean and ugly; from the cowardice that dares not face new truth, the slothfulness contented with half-truths, and the pride that thinks it knows all truth; from all intolerance for other views; from everything in our lives and methods that may hide Thy true light; from the disloyalty of being satisfied with things as they are, in the Church, and in the world; and from failing to share Thy indignation, O Christ, deliver us. (133 and 89)

PETITIONS

Heavenly Father: Grant us so sure a confidence in Thy unfailing sympathy that we may go to Thee whenever we are perplexed or in trouble, to be raised by Thee into that serene faith in which all sorrows are healed and all sins forgiven, and into that abiding peace which the world cannot give or take away. (53 ad)

SPECIAL INTERCESSIONS
FOR CONFIRMANDS

Be pleased, O God of truth, to inspire our confirmands in this church. Prepare their minds and hearts for a decision to live for

Jesus Christ. Help them, and us, to follow closely in the footsteps of Him who trusted fully in Thee and went about doing good. (109)

For Sunday Church Schools

O God, our Father, in whose image all the children of men are made: Most heartily we beseech Thee to bless our Sunday church school, that all members may be instructed in Thy Word, and that Thy likeness may be renewed in their hearts, through the knowledge of Thy dear Son, our Lord. Open the Holy Scriptures, both to those who teach and to those who learn, that the difficulties of the letter may not hide the light of the Spirit. Make all members ready to be taught and willing to obey, that they may find joy and peace in the way of Thy commandments. Enrich the teachers with patient faithfulness and loving wisdom, and send out more laborers, that the young and tender may be nourished and trained to bring forth fruit unto everlasting life. Let Thy truth be manifest from generation to generation, and the whole family of mankind rejoice together in Thy mercy. (48 ad)

For God's Family on Earth

Hear us, O God, as we offer prayer for our families, for our congregation, for fellow Christians everywhere, and for all Thy Kingdom on earth. Give Thy people strength, courage, and hope; increase the faith of all who believe; graciously draw others into the joy of Thy fellowship, and share the light of Thy Holy Spirit with them. (109)

Communion of Saints

We give Thee thanks, O God, for all who have fought the good fight and finished their course and kept the faith, and for those dear to us who are at rest with Thee. And we beseech Thee that we may follow them as they have followed Christ, that we, redeemed and cleansed, may stand with them before Thy throne. Through Jesus Christ our Lord, to whom, with Thee and the Holy Spirit, we ascribe all honor and glory, world without end. Amen. (128)

Offertory Sentences and Prayer

1. " But when you give alms, do not let your left hand know what your right hand is doing, so that your alms may be in secret; and your Father who sees in secret will reward you." *Matt. 6:3, 4, R.S.V.*

2. " The needs are great:
      Our gifts are small.
    But when we share;
      There's enough for all." (73)

All-gracious God: Let the right hand that was lifted up over the five barley loaves itself rest and remain on the humble offering of Thy servants, that it may be multiplied and abound. Through Him whose grace and compassion supply all our needs. Amen. (116 ad)

Suggestion

If an emphasis on stewardship is desired on the Fourth Sunday in Lent, unit 41 may be suggestive.

23. FIFTH LENTEN SERVICE

Color: Violet

For the Choir

O Thou eternal God: Speak to us the word we need, and let Thy Word abide in us until it has wrought Thy holy will. Cleanse, quicken, and refresh our hearts; direct and increase our faith; and grant that we, by worship at this time, may be enabled to see Thee more clearly, to love Thee more deeply, and to serve Thee more faithfully. Amen. (49)

Opening Sentences

1. God shows His love for us in that while we were yet sinners Christ died for us. *Rom. 5:8, R.S.V.*

2. The Lord is in His holy temple: let all the earth keep silence before Him. *Hab. 2:20.*

Invocation

Almighty God, Lord of peace and Giver of rest: Grant to us at eventide the light of Thy countenance, that we may behold Thy glory and grow in Thy likeness. Enable us to know that Thou art good, and that Thy mercy is from everlasting. Be Thou near to us that we may surely find Thee. Through Jesus Christ our Lord. Amen. (76 ad)

General Prayer

THANKS FOR REDEMPTION

O God, our eternal Friend: We thank Thee that the way to Thee and the portals to paradise have been opened by Thy Son, who graciously submitted to mockery, cruelties, and death. Accept our thanks for making redemption and eternal salvation available for each of us. (66 ad)

CONFESSION OF SINS

O most mighty and merciful Father, who hast compassion on all men, and hatest nothing Thou hast made; who desirest not the death of a sinner, but rather that he should turn from his wickedness and live: Mercifully forgive our trespasses; receive and comfort all who are grieved and wearied with the burden of their sins; enable us to overcome all temptations, and henceforth to live a godly, righteous, and sober life. (44)

For Growth

Day by day help us to grow in faith, in self-denial, in love, in heavenly-mindedness, in the purity by which we may see Thee, and the surrender that makes us one with Thee. Inspire us with Divine faith, and subdue us to lowly patience. (88 ad)

Desire to Seek God

Keep alive in us, we beseech Thee, the longing of a child for his father, of the sinner for his Saviour, of the shipwrecked sailor for dry land. Grant that in the stress of business and in meditative hours we may never be far away from Thee. (53 ad)

For the Confirmands

O God: Help us to say with all the seriousness of the confirmands throughout Thy Church: "Lord Jesus, for Thee we live, for Thee we suffer, for Thee we die! Lord Jesus, Thine will we be in life and death! Grant us, O Lord, eternal salvation!" Pour out Thy blessing upon the children of our homes, of our church, and of the whole world. Make Thy light to shine in their hearts more and more, that they may see Thee as their loving Friend and their glorious King, and may follow Jesus Christ as their Master and Redeemer. Help them to overcome temptation through Thy grace. Fill them with the Spirit of Christ that they may be sincere and unselfish; and bring them at last into the glory of the eternal home. (66 ad)

Special Intercessions
For Those in Authority

Because the reins of government are in Thy hands, we beseech Thee to direct and bless all who are in lawful authority; especially Thy servant, the President of the United States, and all others to whom the people have entrusted power, together with the whole body of the Commonwealth. Let Thy Fatherly favor so preserve them, and Thy Holy Spirit so govern their hearts, that religion may be maintained, and our land sustained in righteousness and peace. (127 ab)

For All Nations

Almighty and everlasting God, who hast wrought the redemption of man in a miraculous manner, in sending Thy Son to fulfill the promises made unto our fathers: Help us more and more to spread the knowledge of that salvation, that in all places of the earth Thy truth and power may be made known, so that all nations may praise, honor, and glorify Thee. (26 ad)

For Comfort in Thy Will

Hasten the time when all men shall live and work co-operatively with Thee and each other. Comfort Thy servants now sorrowing over the world; grant them patience and strong confidence in Thy wise rule, that they may continue to trust and hope through the might of Him who said, "Not My will, but Thine, be done." (53 ad)

A Collect for Aid Against Perils

Lighten our darkness, we beseech Thee, O Lord; and by Thy great mercy defend us from all perils and dangers of this night. For the love of Thy only Son, our Saviour, Jesus Christ. Amen. (126)

Offertory Sentences and Prayer

"Therefore do not be anxious, saying, 'What shall we eat?' or 'What shall we drink?' or 'What shall we wear?' For the Gentiles seek all these things; and your Heavenly Father knows that you need them all. But seek first His Kingdom and His righteousness, and all these things shall be yours as well." *Matt. 6:31–33, R.S.V.*

Father in heaven: Accept the gifts that Thy children bring to Thee, and grant that they may be used for Thy glory and the good of Thy Church. (46)

O God, who art great and high and holy: Fill us with Thy love; and give us humble, teachable, and obedient hearts, that we may learn to love Thee truly and serve Thee faithfully. Through Jesus Christ our Lord, to whom, with Thee and the Holy Spirit, we give all glory forever and ever. Amen. (46)

24. FIFTH SUNDAY IN LENT (Judica or Passion)
March 8 to April 11
Color: Violet

Opening Sentences

Come unto Me, all ye that labor and are heavy laden, and I will give you rest. Take My yoke upon you, and learn of Me; for I am meek and lowly in heart: and ye shall find rest unto your souls. For My yoke is easy, and My burden is light. *Matt. 11:28-30.*

Invocation

O Lord, our God, who art the Life of all, the Help of those who flee unto Thee, and the Hope of those who cry unto Thee: Look mercifully upon us! Cleanse our minds and hearts that with a clear conscience and a calm hope we may confidently worship Thee. Through Jesus Christ our Lord. Amen. (5 ad)

Scripture Selections (50, 151, 128)

A —	*Heb.*	9:11-15	Christ the High Priest of Good Things to Come
	John	8:46-59	The Sinlessness of Jesus
E —	*I Peter*	1:17-25	The Precious Blood of Christ
	John	13:31-35	The New Commandment
	Num.	21:4-9	Moses and the Fiery Serpents
P —	*John*	6:27-35	He That Cometh to Me Shall Not Hunger
	Ex.	20:1-22	The Ten Commandments
T —	*Heb.*	7:24-27	Christ's Unchangeable Priesthood
	Heb.	4:14-16	Tempted Like We Are, Yet Without Sin
	John	12:23-33	Jesus Signifies the Manner of His Death

General Prayer

THANKS FOR LIFE AND HOPE

Most gracious God: We thank Thee that Thou hast planted within each of us a knowledge of Thy way and life, and that our hearts are restless till they rest in Thee. We honor Thee for giving us life and hope through the sufferings and death of Thy dear Son. Help us ever to draw nearer to Thee through His cross and ours, granting us comfort and consolation in all our trials and adversities. (139 and 66)

CONFESSION OF SINS

Lord of all might and compassion, who knowest our frame and rememberest our weaknesses: We humbly confess the evil we have done and our weariness in well-doing, the vows we have broken, the duties we have refused, the hours we have lightly spent without any gracious deed, the tasks undone which proclaim us idle and unprofitable servants, and all our many transgressions, shortcomings, and offenses. Have compassion on our unworthiness, we beseech Thee; create in us a sincere desire for whatsoever things are true, just, honorable, pure, and of good report; mold us inwardly to Thy will; so unite us with Thyself in love and confidence that whatever Thou withholdest we may cheerfully resign, whatever Thou commandest we may diligently perform, and whatever Thou bestowest we may gratefully use; and in the end be more than conquerors through Him who loved us and gave Himself for us. (53 ad)

FOR THOSE UNJUSTLY ACCUSED

Give ear, O God, to our several intercessions. Strengthen and support all persons unjustly accused or misunderstood. O Thou, who knowest men's inmost thoughts: Give them grace to pray for all who do them wrong; hear and bless them when they pray. (112 ad)

FOR ALL WHO ARE IN TROUBLE

God of all comfort: We commend unto Thee all who are in any way afflicted — all persons oppressed with poverty, sickness, or other trouble of body or sorrow of mind; and all such as we name in our hearts. Grant them the consolations of which they have need, and overrule their present sufferings to their eternal good. (128 ad)

Special Intercessions
For Confirmands

Remember in Thy great mercy, we beseech Thee, the confirmands in this congregation and throughout Thy Church. By Thy Holy Spirit enlighten and instruct them in the knowledge of Thee and Thy truth. Open their hearts to Thy law day and night. Strengthen and confirm them in the doctrine of Thy grace, and unite them more closely with Thyself and Thy Church. (66 ab)

For the Absent

O God of Love, who art not far away from any of Thy children: Watch with Thy care those who are far away from us; be within their hearts; give them unfailing trust in Thee; grant them power against temptation; make it their joy to do Thy will. Strengthen the bonds of love which unite them to Thee and to us. For the sake of Jesus Christ, who offered Himself without blemish to Thee. Amen. (83 ab)

Offertory Sentence and Prayer

After Jacob's vision at Beth-el, he made a vow, saying, " Of all that Thou shalt give me I will surely give the tenth unto Thee." *Gen. 28:22.*

O God, to whom belongs all that we have: Consecrate in Thy house these material symbols of our labor. Put the touch of Thy hand upon the gifts which we have brought for the ongoing work of Thy people on earth. For Jesus' sake. Amen. (159 ad)

25. SIXTH LENTEN SERVICE

Color: Violet

For the Choir

O Lord, before whose throne stand the heavenly choirs: Bless, we beseech Thee, the ministry of this choir, that those who worship here may with firmer faith seek Thy heavenly Kingdom. Through Jesus Christ our Lord. Amen. (146)

Opening Sentences

Therefore also now, saith the Lord, turn ye even to Me with all your heart. . . . And rend your heart, and not your garments, and turn unto the Lord your God: for He is gracious and merciful, slow to anger, and of great kindness. *Joel 2:12, 13.*

Invocation

O Lord our God, of boundless compassion and infinite love to man: Look down on us and show unto us, and to all who pray with us, the riches of Thy mercy and compassion; and so make us worthy, with a pure heart and a broken spirit, with hallowed lips and with a countenance that needs not to be ashamed, to call upon Thee. Through Jesus Christ our Lord. Amen. (27 ad)

General Prayer

FOR PEACE

Abide with us, O searching and chastening Spirit of the living God, for it is evening and the day is far spent. Let the shadow of Thy presence shelter us from the haste and fret of the day, and the sense of Thy guidance give us peace and rest. (104 ab)

DIRECT US TO THY SON

O Heavenly Father: Help us to profit by the coming of Thy Son, who became our example in faithful and loyal service. Direct our minds to His words, that they may be a power unto salvation, a lamp for our feet, and a light for our path. Cause us to love Him who suffered and died in our place to reconcile us with Thee. Direct our thoughts that we may never forget His agony, humiliation, and death. (66 ad)

INTERCESSION FOR SUFFERERS

O God, who art full of compassion and tender mercy: Hear us as we pray for those who suffer: for all who are handicapped in the race of life through no fault of their own; for the overworked, the hungry, and the destitute; for lonely people who have had to bear heavy burdens; for those who are in doubt and anguish of mind; for those who are oversensitive and afraid; for those whose suffering is unrelieved by the knowledge of Thy love; and for those who suffer through their own wrongdoing. Keep Thy children in all perplexities, griefs, and sorrows; from fear and distrust; that, upheld by Thy strength, they may abide in Thee through all periods of storm and stress. (133 ad)

SPECIAL INTERCESSIONS
A THANKSGIVING

To our prayers, O Lord, we join our hearty thanks for all Thy mercies: for our being, our reason, and all other endowments and faculties of soul and body; for our health, friends, food, and raiment, and all other comforts and conveniences of life. Above all, we adore Thy mercy in sending Thy only Son into the world, to redeem us from sin and eternal death, and in giving us the knowledge and sense of our duty toward Thee. We bless Thee for Thy patience with us, notwithstanding our many and great transgressions; for all the directions, assistances, and comforts of Thy Holy Spirit; for Thy continual care and watchful providence over us through the whole course of our lives; and particularly for the mercies and benefits of the past day; beseeching Thee to give us grace to show our thankfulness in a sincere obedience to His laws, through whose merits and intercession we received them all, Thy Son our Saviour. (126 ad)

Continue Thy Kindness

O God: Continue Thy loving-kindness, that we may rejoice and be glad in Thee all our days. Supply all our needs according to Thy riches, and make all grace to be multiplied in us that we may abound in every good work. Teach us also to make all our requests known unto Thee by prayer and supplication with thanksgiving, that Thy peace, which passes all understanding, may keep our hearts and minds through Jesus Christ, our Lord, to whom with Thee and the Holy Spirit be everlasting honor. Amen. (45 ad)

Offertory Sentence and Prayer

All things whatsoever ye would that men should do to you, do ye even so to them: for this is the law and the prophets. *Matt. 7:12.*

O God, who art the Giver of all good: We give Thee thanks and praise for the bounty of Thy providence and the riches of Thy grace, and we dedicate ourselves to Thee in the love and fellowship of Thy Son our Saviour; in token whereof we present unto Thee this our offering, beseeching Thee graciously to accept and bless it. Through the same Jesus Christ our Lord. Amen. (46)

26. PALM SUNDAY (Sixth Sunday in Lent)
March 15 to April 18 (Sunday Before Easter)
Color: Violet

For the Choir

Almighty God, who hast ever revealed Thyself to mankind through beauty and hast made Thy will known through the ministry of the arts: We thank Thee that Thou hast set apart these choir members to lead Thy people to Thee in worship through music. Give us now the true spirit of praise. For the sake of Jesus Christ. Amen. (79)

Opening Sentences

1. Rejoice greatly, O daughter of Zion; shout, O daughter of Jerusalem: behold, thy King cometh unto thee: He is just, and having salvation; lowly, and riding upon an ass, and upon a colt the foal of an ass. *Zech. 9:9.*

2. Lift up your heads, O ye gates; even lift them up, ye everlasting doors; and the King of glory shall come in. Who is this King of glory? The Lord of Hosts, He is the King of glory. *Ps. 24:9, 10.*

3. The voice of rejoicing and salvation is in the tabernacles of the righteous: . . . Blessed be He that cometh in the Name of the Lord. *Ps. 118:15, 26.*

Invocation

O God: We praise Thee for the Master who rode in triumph into the city of His fathers. We thank Thee that He came not as a conqueror to destroy, but as the Messiah to save. Grant that He may ride on in gentle majesty to win our country, our homes, and our lives for the world-wide brotherhood of man. Enable us in this hour to cast the garments of pride before Him, that in the right spirit every knee shall bow and every tongue confess that Jesus is our Lord, to Thy eternal glory. Amen. (90 ad)

Scripture Selections (50, 157, 151, 128)

A —	*Phil.*	*2:5–11*	The Humiliation and Exaltation of Christ
	Matt.	*21:1–9*	Jesus Enters Jerusalem
	(Episcopalians use *Matt. 27:1–54.*)		
E —	*Heb.*	*12:1–6*	Looking Unto Jesus
	John	*12:1–8*	Mary Anointed Jesus
	Zech.	*9:8–12*	Behold, Thy King Cometh to Thee
P —	*Mark*	*11:1–11*	The Triumphal Entry
	Luke	*19:29–44*	The Triumphal Entry
	Jer.	*7:1–11*	Temple Worship of No Avail to the Ungodly
S —	*Phil.*	*2:12–18*	The Sons of God as Lights in the World
	John	*3:22–36*	John's Witness of Christ
	John	*12:12–19*	Jesus Enters Jerusalem
	Ps.	*8*	God's Great Love to Man

General Prayer

THANKS FOR HUMILIATION AND EXALTATION

We thank Thee, our Saviour, that Thou didst take upon Thyself the form of a servant, humbling Thyself and becoming obedient unto death, even the death of the cross. O Thou who hast been highly exalted, who hast been made King and Lord of glory, enter, we pray Thee, into our hearts. (66 ad)

FOR LOYALTY

Our Father: We have too often been disloyal to the conquering King of this and every day. Forgive us the sins that have brought reproach upon Him and upon Thee. Save us from the fickleness that one day cries hosanna and the next day follows fearfully. When the call of duty sounds, help us to set our faces steadfastly toward our Jerusalem, whether the path be made with palms and flowers, or whether it lead by the way of some cross. (90 ad)

FOR AN INCREASE IN GODLINESS

O Lord: Increase in us faith and devotion; replenish our hearts with all goodness, and by Thy great mercy keep us in the same.

Give us godly zeal in prayer, true humility in prosperity, perfect patience in adversity, and continual joy in the Holy Spirit. (16 ad)

For Church People

O God: To them that teach grant the gifts of knowledge, discernment, and love; to them that minister in holy things to be humble, tender, and pure; to all pastors of Thy flock to be zealous, vigilant, and unworldly, having their hearts set upon invisible things. Grant to our heads of families to be wise and gentle; to our young people to be prudent and chaste; to our old people to be cheerful and fervent; to all engaged in business to be honest and unselfish. Build us up in faith, hope, charity, and all virtues. (125 ab)

Special Intercessions
For Those to Be Confirmed

God of all majesty, infinite power and glory, who hast made Thy ways known to men by Thy Holy Spirit: We rejoice as we call to mind those who have set examples for us; we thank Thee that we have had the privilege of learning and walking in the light, and that there have been young people in our church who were willing to study that they might learn Thy will, confess Thy wisdom, and walk in Thy way. Grant to them growth in Thy grace and knowledge, and help them to make a good confession before men. (109)

An Intercession and Petition

Have mercy upon everyone, O God. Remember every soul who, being in any affliction, trouble, or agony, stands in need of Thy mercy and help; all who are in necessity or distress; all who love or hate us. Lord, be Thou within us, to strengthen us; above us, to protect us; beneath us, to uphold us; before us, to direct us; behind us, to keep us from straying; round about us, to defend us. Through Jesus Christ our Lord. Amen. (2 ad)

Offertory Sentence and Prayer

The point is this: he who sows sparingly will also reap sparingly, and he who sows bountifully will also reap bountifully. *II Cor. 9:6, R.S.V.*

Lord of all worlds: Give us grace to give freely of our possessions as Thou hast need of them. Accept these offerings which we Thy children make to Thee, and grant that the cause to which they are devoted shall be a blessing to men for the glory of Thy Name. Amen. (116 and 90)

27. MAUNDY THURSDAY (Seventh Lenten Service)

Thursday or Wednesday Before Easter

Color: Violet (White if Holy Communion, Recommended in 156 for Maundy Thursday)

A Holy Week Collect for Christian Unity

Eternal God, who art ready to make Thyself near to each of us, especially in the cross of Christ: Gather Thy people from all churches at the foot of His cross where we may learn of Him and unite in obedience to His holy will. Through the same Jesus Christ our Lord. Amen. (109)

Opening Sentences

1. Blessed are they which do hunger and thirst after righteousness: for they shall be filled. *Matt. 5:6.*

2. He hath made His wonderful works to be remembered: Jehovah is gracious and merciful. He hath given food unto them that fear Him. He will ever be mindful of His covenant. *Ps. 111:4, 5, A.S.V.*

Invocation

Most holy and most merciful God, our Heavenly Father: Help us to meditate and pray beneath the shadow of His cross, in the light of His revelation, in the communion of His Spirit, and in the fellowship of His Church. Impress and quicken our hearts with the memory of our Master and Saviour till we learn to feel it to be no task to serve Him, no hardship to follow Him, and no burden to carry His cross in our world. In Jesus' Name. Amen. (76 ad)

Collect

O Lord God, who hast left unto us in a wonderful Sacrament a memorial of Thy Passion: Grant, we beseech Thee, that we may so use this Sacrament of Thy Body and Blood, that the fruits of Thy redemption may continually be manifest in us; who livest and reignest with the Father and the Holy Ghost [Spirit], ever one God, world without end. Amen. (57)

Scripture Selections (50, 151, 128)

A —	*I Cor.*	*11:23–32*	The Lord's Supper
	John	*13:1–15*	Jesus Washes His Disciples' Feet
E —	*I Cor.*	*10:16, 17*	The Essential Communion Blessings
	Luke	*22:14–20*	Christ Institutes His Holy Supper
	Ps.	*111*	Praise of God's Works
P —	*Matt.*	*26:17–30*	The Lord's Supper
	Luke	*23:1–49*	Jesus Before Pilate and Herod. The Crucifixion
T —	*I Cor.*	*10:16, 17*	The Cup of Blessing
	Ex.	*12:1–14*	The Passover Instituted

General Prayer

Direct Us to Thy Passion

O Lord Jesus Christ, our Saviour: Direct our thoughts to Thy holy Passion. Mercifully keep us that we may never esteem lightly the great blessing of Holy Communion which Thou didst institute on the night Thou wast betrayed. Awaken in us a holy sincerity to examine ourselves penitently and conscientiously; and grant that through this holy Sacrament our faith may be increased, our love strengthened, and our salvation established in eternal life. As Thou didst humbly kneel to worship the Father, so make us humble before Thee, that we may renounce all pride and selfishness. Help us to watch and pray that we may not enter into temptation. (66 ad)

Strengthen Us in Prayer

O Lord Jesus Christ, who as on this day didst withdraw Thyself in communion with Thy Father, to prepare for Thy agony and Passion, that, when the tempter should come, he might find nothing in Thee: Give grace unto us, that we too in quiet seasons of meditation and prayer may obtain strength for every trial of our faith. Make us one with Thee in trust, in patience, and in sacrifice, that in every struggle with temptation we may be made more than conquerors. (107 ad)

For Love

O God of Love, who hast given a new commandment through Thy only-begotten Son, that we should love one another, even as Thou didst love us, and gavest Thy beloved Son for our life and salvation: Give to us, Thy servants, in all times of our life on earth, a pure conscience and a sincere mind, a memory forgetful of past ill will, and a heart to love our fellow men. (6 ad)

For the Mind of Christ

More and more let the same mind be in us which was also in Christ Jesus, that we may look for no final peace without the cross. O God, in whose hands our little lives are held: Consecrate our lives to Thy will, giving us such purity of heart, such depth of faith, such steadfastness of purpose that, in Thy good time, we may come to think Thy own thoughts after Thee. (88 and 93)

Give us grace to serve one another in all lowliness, according to the perfect example of Jesus Christ, that we may enter into the fellowship of His sufferings. (101 and 131)

For Others

We call to mind, O God, before Thy throne of grace, all those whom Thou hast given to be near and dear to us, beseeching Thee to remember them all for good and to fulfill, as may be expedient for them and pleasing with Thee, their desires and wants. (12)

For the Increase of the Ministry

O Almighty God: Look mercifully upon the world which Thou hast redeemed by the blood of Thy dear Son, and incline the hearts of many to dedicate themselves to the sacred ministry of Thy Church. (126 ab)

Special Intercessions
A Collect for Peace

O God, from whom all holy desires, all good counsels, and all just works do proceed: Give unto Thy servants that peace which the world cannot give, that our hearts may be set to obey Thy commandments, and also that by Thee, we, being defended from the fear of our enemies, may pass our time in rest and quietness. Through the merits of Jesus Christ our Saviour. Amen. (9)

Offertory Sentence and Prayer

For you know the grace of our Lord Jesus Christ, that though He was rich, yet for your sake He became poor, so that by His poverty you might become rich. *II Cor. 8:9, R.S.V.*

Almighty God, our Heavenly Father, from whom comes every good and perfect gift: We call to remembrance Thy loving-kindness; with grateful hearts we lift up to Thee the voice of our thanksgiving. Stir up, we beseech Thee, the wills of Thy faithful people, that we who have freely received of Thy bounty may always of Thy bounty freely give. Through Jesus Christ our Lord. Amen. (61 ad)

28. GOOD FRIDAY (Eighth Lenten Service)
The Friday Before Easter
Color: Black

For the Choir

O God of compassion, whose love is unending: Inspire us as we stand in readiness, that we may be filled with adoration and praise. Be with everyone whose voice is raised and whose knee is bent, and we will ascribe all honor and glory to Thee. Through Jesus Christ our Redeemer. Amen. (109)

Opening Sentences

1. Is it nothing to you, all ye that pass by? behold, and see if there be any sorrow like unto My sorrow, which is done unto Me, wherewith the Lord hath afflicted Me. *Lam. 1:12.*

2. "Worthy is the Lamb who was slain, to receive power and wealth and wisdom and might and honor and glory and blessing!" *Rev. 5:12, R.S.V.*

3. Surely He hath borne our griefs, and carried our sorrows: yet we did esteem Him stricken, smitten of God, and afflicted. But He was wounded for our transgressions, He was bruised for our iniquities: the chastisement of our peace was upon Him; and with His stripes we are healed. *Isa. 53:4, 5.*

Invocation

Almighty God: Graciously behold Thy Church, for which Thy Son suffered death upon the cross; and grant that our hearts may be so fixed on Him with steadfast faith that we may worship Thee more deeply and receive the forgiveness of our sins. In the Name of Jesus Christ our Lord. Amen. (66 ab)

Invocation and Confession (Evening)

O Thou whose chosen dwelling is the heart that longs for Thy presence and humbly seeks Thy face: We come to Thee as the day declines and the shadows of evening fall. Deepen within us the sense of shame and sorrow for the wrongs we have done, for the good we have left undone; and strengthen every desire to amend our lives according to Thy holy will. Restore unto us the joy of Thy salvation; bind up that which is broken; give light to our minds, strength to our wills, and rest to our souls. According to Thy loving-kindness in Jesus Christ our Lord. Amen. (128)

Scripture Selections (50, 151, 128)

A —	*Isa.*	*52:13 to 53:12*	Surely He Has Borne Our Griefs
	John,	*chs. 18; 19*	The Crucifixion of Our Lord
E —	*II Cor.*	*5:14–21*	Reconciliation Through Christ
	Luke	*23:39–46*	The Crucifixion
	Ps.	*22:1–19*	My God, Why Hast Thou Forsaken Me?
P —	*Mark*	*15:15–39*	Jesus Mocked and Crucified
	Ps.	22	A Cry of Anguish and a Song of Praise
T —	*Heb.*	*10:19–23*	The New and Living Way
	Matt.	*27:29–56*	Death and Burial of Jesus

General Prayer

PRAISE FOR HIS PASSION

Almighty and most merciful Father, who, in compassion for Thy children, didst give Thy holy and spotless Son to bear their sins in His body on the tree: We bless Thee for the love made known in Him, and for the redemption sealed to us by His perfect sacrifice. We thank Thee for the burdens He bore, the pains He suffered, the words of comfort He spoke; for His bitter conflict with the powers of darkness, and His eternal victory over sin and death. Blessing, and honor, and glory, and power, be unto Thee, O God, and unto the Lamb, forever and ever. (107)

LOOK MERCIFULLY

Look mercifully upon us, we beseech Thee, as before His cross we meditate and pray; give us faith so to behold Him in the mystery of His Passion that we may enter into the fellowship of His sufferings.

Let His wounds be our healing, His cross our redemption, and His death our life. (107 ab)

A Prayer in the Form of the Seven Words

Lord Jesus: Behold us as we in spirit gather around Thy cross and marvel at the mystery of Thy wonderful love. O let the sacred seven words, which Thou didst speak when dying, become Divine power and wisdom in our souls. Our merciful High Priest! As Thou on the cross didst ask forgiveness for Thy enemies, intercede for us as our sympathizing advocate. O Lamb of God, who art taking away the sin of the world: Have mercy upon us and give us Thy peace. Implant in our hearts the virtues of gentleness and patience, that we may love our enemies, rejoice in Thy love, and overcome evil with good. Grant us a vision of Thy Kingdom of grace and glory, whenever we repent and call on Thee, as did the malefactor at Thy side. Subdue the hardest heart and bring all wanderers home. As dying Thou didst unite Thy mother with Thy beloved disciple, so unite us with our kindred in the bonds of love and peace. (66) Cause Thy Spirit to reign in the homes of all Thy children. (126) Help us to love the poor, protect the oppressed, and comfort the sad. (66) O Thou who wast forsaken of God because of our iniquity, forsake us not when our souls long for comfort. In loneliness make us aware of Thy presence; in unpopularity make us steadfast to the best we know; in temptation send us Thy still small voice. (66 and 89) O blessed Jesus, our Lord and Master, who wast pleased to thirst for our souls, grant that we may not be satisfied with the pleasures of this lower life, but ever thirst for the souls Thou didst die to save, and, above all, to thirst for Thee. (80 ab) Strengthen our faith in the redemptive work Thou hast finished. We thank Thee for the means of grace and the hope of glory. Thou great Shepherd of the sheep, gather the sheep still outside the fold, that every knee may bow before Thee and every tongue confess that Thou art Lord. Help us to trust in Thy all-sufficient sacrifice, that we may commend our spirit into Thy hands, yea, into the hands of the Father. Keep us through faith and bring us to Thy everlasting Kingdom and glory. (66 ad)

For Reconciliation

O Lord Jesus Christ, who didst hang upon the cross that all mankind might be saved: Draw us to Thyself; nourish us with Thy life, and make us followers in Thy ministry of reconciliation. To our families and all bound to us by ties of kinship and affection, give us loyalty and gratitude. Toward our comrades and associates give us reverence and appreciation. Toward all who are separated from us by circumstances of life, help us to feel our true sense of brotherhood. Toward the ill, the underpaid, the underfed; toward all who toil beyond their strength, all who carry crushing burdens; toward all classes and nations and races, grant us Thy ministry of healing and strength. (89 ad)

Special Intercessions
For Those in Extremity

Most merciful God, who art a seasonable refuge in time of trouble: Let the prayers of those who, in tribulation or any sort of extremity, cry unto Thee reach Thy merciful ears, and grant them relief according to their several necessities, giving them patience under their sufferings, and a happy issue out of all their afflictions. For the sake of the suffering and sorrow of Thy dear Son, our Saviour, Jesus Christ. Amen. (50)

Offertory Sentences and Prayer

1. Give unto the Lord the glory due unto His Name: bring an offering, and come into His courts. *Ps. 96:8.*

2. Let us run with patience the race that is set before us, looking unto Jesus the Author and Finisher of our faith; who for the joy that was set before Him endured the cross, despising the shame, and is set down at the right hand of the throne of God. *Heb. 12:1, 2.*

O God, who dost love us with an everlasting love: Help us ever to remember and give thanks to Thee — through sacrificial gifts and deeds — in the blessed imitation of Thy Son, who gave His life for us all. Bless these gifts and all givers for Jesus' sake. Amen. (139 ad)

29. EASTER
March 22 to April 25
Liturgical Color: White

For the Choir
Eternal Father, who hast made us that our chief joy may be in Thee: Be pleased of Thy great mercy to sanctify us in thought and feeling, and to free us from the power of this present world, that in quietness and holiness we may worship Thee; show forth Thy praise not only with our lips, but in our lives; and live before Thee in faith and righteousness all our days. Through Jesus Christ our Lord. Amen. (124)

Opening Sentences
1. "He [Jesus Christ] has risen." *Mark 16:6, R.S.V.*
"The Lord has risen indeed." *Luke 24:34, R.S.V.*
"Death is swallowed up in victory." . . . Thanks be to God, who gives us the victory through our Lord Jesus Christ. *I Cor. 15:54, 57, R.S.V.*

2. "Fear not, I am the first and the last, and the living One; I died, and behold I am alive for evermore, and I have the keys of Death and Hades." *Rev. 1:17, 18, R.S.V.*
Lo, I am with you alway, even unto the end of the world. *Matt. 28:20.*

3. Christ our passover is sacrificed for us: Therefore let us keep the feast, not with old leaven, neither with the leaven of malice and wickedness; but with the unleavened bread of sincerity and truth. *I Cor. 5:7, 8.*

4. To this end Christ died and lived again, that He might be Lord both of the dead and of the living. *Rom. 14:9, R.S.V.*

Invocation
Almighty God, who through the death of Thy Son didst overcome sin and death, and through His resurrection hast brought to light

life and immortality, that we, redeemed from the power of Satan, might live in Thy Kingdom: Help us, we beseech Thee, to believe with all our hearts the blessed story of the resurrection, to abide in this faith continually, and to bless and praise Thee always. Through Jesus Christ, Thy Son, our Lord. Amen. (66)

Scripture Selections (50, 151, 132, 128)

A —	*Col.*	*3:1–11*	If Ye Be Risen
	Mark	*16:1–8*	The Resurrection of Our Lord
	(Lutherans list *I Cor.* 5:6–8.)		
E —	*I Cor.*	*15:12–20*	Christ Is Risen from the Dead
	Matt.	*28:1–10*	The Women at the Sepulcher
	Ps.	*118:14–24*	The Right Hand of the Lord Is Exalted
P —	*Rev.*	*1:10–18*	I Was Dead, and, Behold, I Am Alive
	John	*20:1–10*	The Resurrection of Our Lord
T —	*I Peter*	*1:3–9*	Receiving the End of Our Faith
	Job	*19:22–27*	I Know that My Redeemer Liveth
S —	*Acts*	*13:26–39*	Paul's Easter Sermon at Antioch
	Luke	*24:1–12*	The Resurrection of the Lord

General Prayer

Thanksgiving

O God Most High: All praise and thanksgiving be unto Thee for the multitude of Thy loving-kindness and tender mercies to us and to all men. Today we praise Thee for the glorious resurrection of Thy Son Jesus Christ our Lord, who hath taken away the sins of the world; who by His death hath destroyed death; and by His rising again hath brought us to everlasting life. (128 ad)

We give Thee thanks that, having overcome the sharpness of death, He opened the Kingdom of Heaven to all believers; and that because He liveth, we too shall live. Even now, having peace with Thee through Him, we rejoice in the hope of Thy great glory. Thanks be to Thee, O God, who givest us the victory through our Lord Jesus Christ. (128 ab)

SUPPLICATION

O God, who through the mighty resurrection of Thy Son Jesus Christ from the dead hast delivered us from the power of darkness into the Kingdom of Thy love: Grant, we beseech Thee, that as by His death He hath recalled us into life, so by His presence ever abiding in us He may raise us to joys eternal. Through Him who for our sakes died and rose again, and is ever with us in power and great glory. (128 ab)

INTERCESSIONS

Almighty God, whose blessed Son Christ Jesus sent forth His apostles to make disciples of all nations: Fill Thy Church throughout the world with His risen power. Pour out Thy Spirit on those who are called to minister in His Name, at home and abroad. As they break the bread of life to others, let their own souls be nourished and sustained. Grant to Thy people here and everywhere that, abiding in Christ their Life, they may bear fruit abundantly to Thy glory. (128)

O God, who hast promised Thy Son the uttermost parts of the earth for His possession: Take away the veil from all hearts that they may behold the Messiah from of old, and hasten the day when all peoples shall know Him as Saviour and worship Him as Lord. (128)

FOR OUR LAND

Let Thy mercy, we beseech Thee, rest upon our land and nation, upon all in authority, that there may be justice and peace at home and that we may show forth Thy praise among the nations of the earth. Break the power of unbelief and superstition, and preserve to us Thy pure Word, in its liberty and glory, to the end of our days. (128)

FOR ALL WHO ARE AFFLICTED

O Heavenly Father: We commend to Thy merciful care all who are in any way afflicted. Relieve those who suffer; restore health and strength, as Thou dost will, to those who are sick. In Christ, who is the Resurrection and the Life, let the heavy-laden find strength to endure and those who are in the valley of the shadow see the light of life eternal. Give to those in sorrow or loneliness the assurance that nothing can ever separate them from Thy love, which is in Christ Jesus. (128 ad)

SPECIAL INTERCESSIONS
COMMUNION OF SAINTS

Almighty God, who hast knit together Thy elect in one communion and fellowship, in the mystical Body of Thy Son Christ our Lord: Grant us grace so to follow Thy blessed saints in all virtuous and godly living that we may come to those unspeakable joys which Thou hast prepared for those who love Thee. Through the same Thy Son Jesus Christ our Lord, to whom, with Thee the Father and the Holy Spirit, be all honor and glory, world without end. Amen. (128 ad)

Alternate General Prayer
THANKS FOR THY RESURRECTION

Our blessed Redeemer and Lord, Jesus Christ, who didst come forth as the beautiful dawn of a new day: We thank and praise Thee for Thy glorious resurrection. O Thou who art the Resurrection and the Life, abide with us, that in our lives we may praise and bless Thee for Thy love and mercy. (66)

MAKE US PARTAKERS

O Lord Jesus Christ: Make us partakers of Thy great victory, and of all the glorious fruits of Thy death and resurrection. Grant that we may no longer live in sin to ourselves, but live to Thee, who hast died and art risen again for us. On this anniversary of Thy great victory we beseech Thee so to strengthen us in faith that we may never doubt that Thou hast conquered sin, Satan, and death. Give us, we pray Thee, the blessed assurance that we also may conquer, and day by day walk in the newness of life. Grant to us the assurance of our faith, amid all the sorrows, trials, and temptations of our mortal state, and especially when we walk in the valley of the shadow of death, that there is reserved for us in heaven an inheritance incorruptible and undefiled, which fades not away, and that our graves shall verify Thy glorious truth, "I am the Resurrection, and the Life." (66 ad and 128)

For Grace to Follow

O Christ, who didst rise in triumph from the grave and didst bear in Thy pierced hands the keys of hell and death: Teach us to look and see Thee standing on the everlasting shores of peace, and suffer us to come through the waters. Give us grace, O Lord our God, to arise and leave all and follow Thee all our days. (139 ad)

For Others

Grant that the Easter message of Thy glorious resurrection may strengthen the hearts of all who struggle with temptation or with the trials and sorrows of life. May they be comforted by Thy victory. Have mercy upon all who have not yet felt the power of Thy resurrection and are still dead in sin. Awaken them through Thy Holy Spirit, that they may leave the dark tomb of sin and walk before Thee in the newness of life. According to Thy rich mercy, remember the sick and the dying; refresh their languishing hearts and comfort them with the Word of life. Teach them to say, " I know that my Redeemer liveth." Make their tears give way to joy and their sighs to Thy praise. (66 ad)

Special Intercessions
A Closing Prayer of Praise

O Father of our Lord Jesus Christ, who hast brought again from the dead the great Shepherd of the sheep: Make us perfect in every good thing to do Thy will, working in us that which is pleasing in Thy sight, through Jesus Christ, Thy Son, to whom with Thee and the Holy Spirit, be praise and glory, age after age. Amen. (*Heb. 13:20, 21,* as ad in 66)

Offertory Sentence and Prayers

" Do not lay up for yourselves treasures on earth, where moth and rust consume and where thieves break in and steal, but lay up for yourselves treasures in heaven, where neither moth nor rust consumes and where thieves do not break in and steal; for where your treasure is, there will your heart be also." *Matt. 6:19–21, R.S.V.*

1. O Lord God, our Heavenly Father, who hast delivered up Thy

Son for our sins and raised Him for our justification: Accept these special gifts which we render to Thee as expressions of our devotion; lead, guide, and keep us in the true faith. Through Thy Son, our living Lord. (66 ad)

2. O God, our Heavenly Father, who hast set Thy servants in the world to continue the blessed ministry of our risen Saviour Jesus Christ: Be pleased to bless these gifts and all our efforts to spread the good news. Hasten the day of triumph when the kingdoms of the world shall become the Kingdom of our glorious Lord. Amen. (32)

Alternate Benediction for Eastertide

Now the God of peace, that brought again from the dead our Lord Jesus, that great Shepherd of the sheep, through the blood of the everlasting covenant, make you perfect in every good work to do His will, working in you that which is well-pleasing in His sight, through Jesus Christ; to whom be glory for ever and ever. Amen. *Heb. 13:20, 21.*

30. FIRST SUNDAY AFTER EASTER (Quasimodogeniti)
March 29 to May 2
Liturgical Color: White

For the Choir

O God of peace: Fill our hearts with faith, that with joy and thanksgiving we may remember His triumph over death. Inspire us in all our efforts to praise Thee. In the Name of Him who brought newness of life. Amen. (109)

Opening Sentence

If ye then be risen with Christ, seek those things which are above, where Christ sitteth on the right hand of God. *Col. 3:1.*

Invocation

O God: We invoke Thy presence with us as we seek to worship Thee, that we may lay aside our worldly thoughts and plans, and fix our hearts on Thee alone; that we, being refreshed and strengthened, purified and comforted, may love Thee more sincerely and serve Thee more devotedly. Through Jesus Christ our Lord. Amen. (116 ab)

Scripture Selections (50, 157, 151, 128)

A —	*I John*	*5:4-12*	The Victory That Overcomes
	John	*20:19-31*	Thomas Incredulous
	(Episcopalians: *John 20:19-23.*)		
E —	*I Peter*	*1:3-9*	Receiving the End of Our Faith
	John	*21:15-19*	Reinstatement of Peter
	Gen.	*32:21-30*	Jacob Wrestles with the Angel
P —	Rom.	*6:1-14*	Dead Unto Sin, but Alive Unto God
	Luke	*24:36-49*	Jesus Appears in Jerusalem
	Ps.	*103*	Bless the Lord, O My Soul

General Prayer

A General Thanksgiving

Almighty God, Father of all mercies: We, Thy unworthy servants, do give Thee most humble and hearty thanks for all Thy goodness and loving-kindness to us, and to all men. We praise Thee for our creation, preservation, and all the blessings of this life; but above all, for Thy wonderful love in the redemption of the world by our Lord Jesus Christ; for the means of grace, and for the hope of glory. And, we beseech Thee, give us a due sense of all Thy mercies, that our hearts may be sincerely thankful; and that we shall show forth Thy praise, not only with our lips, but in our lives, by giving ourselves to Thy service, and by walking before Thee in holiness and righteousness all our days. (126 ad)

For the New Life

O Lord and our God, who hast taught us the blessedness of believing even though we have not seen: We thank Thee for the power that overcomes the world, even our faith, through which we have newness of life and strength. Graciously grant us Thy peace, which the world cannot give or take away, and send us forth to do Thy will. (109)

A Prayer for the Church Universal

O Thou God and Father of our Lord Jesus Christ, of whom the whole family in heaven and earth is named: Cause Thy blessing, we beseech Thee, to rest upon the Church, which He hath redeemed with His most precious blood. Enlighten its ministers with true knowledge and understanding of Thy Word. Send down Thy grace upon all its congregations. Deliver it from false doctrine, heresy, and schism; enable it to keep the unity of the spirit in the bond of peace, and clothe it with the beauty of holiness. Establish and reveal Thy glory among all nations. By the working of Thy providence, confound and destroy all wicked devices against Thy holy Word, and bring in speedily the full victory of Thy everlasting Kingdom. (50 ad)

SPECIAL INTERCESSIONS
A PRAYER FOR ALL CONDITIONS OF MEN

O God, the Creator and Preserver of all mankind: We implore Thy mercy in behalf of all classes and conditions of men, that it may please Thee to visit them with Thy most compassionate help, according to their manifold necessities and wants. Especially do we beseech Thee to have pity upon all widows and orphans; upon all prisoners and captives; upon all sick and dying persons; upon all such as are persecuted for righteousness' sake. Enable them to look unto Thee, O most merciful Father, and to call upon Thy Name, that they may find a present Saviour in their affliction and distress. And let it please Thee to deliver them, and raise them up in due time, giving them patience under all their sufferings, the rich comfort of Thy grace here below, and eternal rest with Thee in heaven. Through Jesus Christ our Lord. Amen. (126 as ad in 50)

Offertory Sentence and Prayer

He who contributes, in liberality; he who gives aid, with zeal; he who does acts of mercy, with cheerfulness. *Rom. 12:8, R.S.V.*

Receive, O Lord, we pray Thee, these our offerings which we render for the service of Thy Church, and accept with them our hearts and lives, which we consecrate anew to Thee. Through Jesus Christ our Lord. Amen. (113 ab)

Suggestion

Mother's Day, or Festival of the Christian Home (unit 42), Memorial Day Sunday (unit 43), and Rural Life Sunday (unit 32) may be celebrated in May.

31. SECOND SUNDAY AFTER EASTER (Misericordias Domini)

April 5 to May 9

Liturgical Color: White

For the Choir

O gracious God, who art pleased when Thy children enter into Thy presence with thanksgiving: We thank Thee for the high and holy privilege we have of leading the congregation in worship. Bless each of us, according to our needs and the riches of Thy mercy, that unitedly we may give glory to Thee in sincerity and reverence. Through Jesus Christ our Lord. Amen. (109)

Opening Sentences

1. O come, let us worship and bow down: let us kneel before the Lord our Maker. For He is our God; and we are the people of His pasture, and the sheep of His hand. *Ps. 95:6, 7.*

2. So we Thy people and sheep of Thy pasture will give Thee thanks for ever: we will show forth Thy praise to all generations. *Ps. 79:13.*

Invocation

O God, the Inspirer of our common worship, and the Reward of all our seeking: Visit, we pray Thee, this congregation and each of us with Thy indwelling Spirit. Unite us in fellowship with Thy worshipers in all lands; and grant that our thoughts and words and the unspoken longings of our hearts may be acceptable in Thy sight, and may be offered in the Name of our Master, Jesus Christ. Amen. (89)

Scripture Selections (50, 157, 151, 128)

A — *I Peter* 2:21–25 You Were as Sheep Going Astray

John 10:11–16 The Good Shepherd

(Episcopalians: *I Peter* 2:19–25.)

E — *Eph.*	*2:4–10*	The Riches of God's Grace
John	*14:1–6*	The Way, the Truth, and the Life
Ps.	*23*	The Lord Is My Shepherd
P — *Rev.*	*21:10–14, 21–27*	The Holy City, Jerusalem
John	*10:1–10*	The Parable of the Sheepfold

General Prayer

REJOICING IN GOD'S POWER

Almighty God, Author of life and Lord of heaven and earth: We praise Thee for all Thy deeds of strength and glory. We sincerely thank Thee for sending Thy compassionate Son into this world of sin, sorrow, and death, and especially for His power to bring back life and hope. Accept our undying gratitude for the promise of a reunion with loved ones in a house not made with hands, but eternal in the heavens. Grant that Thy whole Church in heaven and on earth may continue, through the quickening and life-giving power of Thy Son, to glorify Thee. (109)

FOR THE PRESIDENT AND ALL OTHERS IN AUTHORITY

Almighty God, whose Kingdom is an everlasting kingdom and whose dominion endures throughout all generations: We pray Thee to look with favor upon Thy servants, the President of the United States, the Governor of this state, and all others in authority. Fill them with the spirit of wisdom, goodness, and truth, and so rule their hearts and bless their endeavors that law and order, justice and peace, may everywhere prevail. Preserve us from national sins and corruption. Make us strong and great in the fear of Thee and in the love of righteousness, reverent in the use of freedom, just in the exercise of power, generous in the protection of weakness, that we may become a blessing to all nations. (50 ad)

FOR THE LIVING CHURCH

O Lord God, who dwellest on high and yet delightest to have Thy habitation in the hearts of men: We thank Thee that Thou hast built Thy Church as a city set upon a hill, and laid the foundations of it upon the apostles and prophets, Jesus Christ being the chief cornerstone; make us to be a spiritual building fit for the indwelling of Thy Holy Spirit, grounding us in faith, building us up in hope, and perfecting us in love, after the pattern of Jesus Christ, the Good Shepherd, that we, joined in the union of the Church Militant upon earth, may enter into Thy Church Triumphant in heaven. (25 ad)

SPECIAL INTERCESSIONS
FOR GUIDANCE

O Jesus Christ, our Master: Do Thou meet us while we walk in the way, and long to reach the better country; so that, following Thy light, we may keep in the path of righteousness while Thou, who art the Way, the Truth, and the Life, art guiding us. (129)

FOR OTHERS

Guide and strengthen all Thy people in every church. Help each of us to become more active for the spiritual and temporal welfare of others. Give us insight and grace that we may be what our Saviour was in the world: the sacrificial Servant of the needy, the Seeker of lost sheep, and the Friend of all. (109)

FOR THOSE ABOUT TO BE CONFIRMED

O God, who through the teaching of Thy Son Jesus Christ didst prepare the disciples for the coming of the Comforter: Make ready, we beseech Thee, the hearts and minds of Thy servants who at this time are seeking the Holy Spirit through the laying on of hands, that, drawing near with penitent and faithful hearts, they may evermore be filled with the power of His Divine indwelling. (126 ab)

FOR CHURCH UNITY

Give unto all who seek Thy good pleasure such grace that the bonds of peace in the unity of the Spirit may be kept. And grant most speedily a vision to Thy children of the good they may do if they unite in strength against the powers of evil. Inspire Thy Churches to unite in essential matters, according to Thy Fatherly desires. Help the Church, like a mighty army, to move with power against all that is wrong and unfair; and empower us in every good thing to do Thy will. (109)

These prayers we offer in the Name of Thy Son, that the day may soon come when there shall be one flock throughout the world, under one Shepherd. Amen. (109)

Offertory Sentences and Prayer

1. Honor the Lord with thy substance, and with the firstfruits of all thine increase. *Prov. 3:9.*

2. "We must work the works of Him who sent Me, while it is day; night comes, when no one can work." *John 9:4, R.S.V.*

O God: Let Thy favor be upon these gifts and the cause for which they are given. Increase our love for the Church, and give us a growing understanding of its world-wide task. Keep our feet in the path of duty, and our minds in the love of Christ our Lord. Amen. (148 ad)

32. FIFTH SUNDAY AFTER EASTER (Rogate) (Rural Life Sunday)

April 26 to May 30
Color: White

For the Choir

O God, to whom the cherubim and seraphim adoringly sing: Grant that as our voices are uplifted in this service to Thy praise, so we may continually sing and make melody in our hearts to Thee. Through Jesus Christ our Lord. Amen. (120)

Opening Sentences

1. Rest in the Lord, and wait patiently for him: . . . Delight thyself also in the Lord; and He shall give thee the desires of thine heart. *Ps. 37:7, 4.*

2. Exalt the Lord our God, and worship at His holy hill; for the Lord our God is holy. *Ps. 99:9.*

Invocation

O Lord our God, who art always more ready to bestow Thy good gifts upon us than we are to seek them: Help us so to seek that we may truly find, so to ask that we may joyfully receive, so to knock that the door of Thy mercy may be opened to us. Through Jesus Christ our Lord. Amen. (47)

Scripture Selections (50, 157, 139)

A —	*James*	*1:22–27*	Be Doers of the Word
	John	*16:23–30*	You Shall Ask in My Name
	(Episcopalians are referred to *John 16:23–33.*)		
O —	*Gen.*	*41:39–57*	Joseph Becomes Lord of All Egypt
	Ps.	*65*	God's Abundant Favor to Earth and Man
	Ps.	*95*	Let Us Worship and Bow Down

General Prayer

A Prayer of Thanksgiving

O God, the Giver of every good and every perfect gift: We thank Thee that in Thy mercy Thou hast given us a place among Thy people, and hast enabled us to come to Thy house to worship Thee. We praise Thee for the world in which Thou hast placed us; for the works of Thy hand, which show forth Thy infinite power and unsearchable wisdom. We bless Thee for Thy gifts of reason and understanding whereby we can receive and apprehend their teaching. We thank Thee for the discipline of life; for our Christian upbringing; and for all the experiences that have drawn us nearer to Thee. We praise Thee that Thou hast shown unto us in Jesus Christ Thy Son the pattern of what we ought to be. We thank Thee for the beauty of His life; for His victory over temptation; for the atonement of His death; for His triumph over the grave; for His ascension to Thy right hand; and for His rule over all things. (161 ad)

Bless the Seed

O God, who art the Lord of springtime and harvest: We beseech Thee to bless the seed sown in the earth for the sustenance of mankind. So water it with the gentle rain from heaven and warm it with the golden sunshine that it may bear fruit a hundredfold, to the glory of Thy holy Name and the welfare of Thy people. (111 ad)

Special Intercessions
For the Nearness of the Father

Almighty God, Father of our Lord Jesus Christ, and through Him our Heavenly Father: We rejoice that we may come confidently to Thee for all things needed in the service of Thy Son. We praise and thank Thee for being near to all Thy servants who ask blessings in our Saviour's Name and for His sake. (109)

Grant Us a Pure Religion

Grant to us, dear Father in heaven, a pure religion. Give each of us the spirit of gentleness and love for our fellow men. Guard our hearts and minds that we may control our words and deeds. Ever give to us the desire to practice mercy among the needy. (109)

For the Right Use of Sunday

Lord, who dost ask of Thy people love for love, and worship in return for life: Assist us to keep holy, week by week, the day of Thy Son's mighty rising from the dead, and bless us in the breaking of bread and the offering of prayers, that others of Thy children who behold our joy may seek Thy loving-kindness in the midst of Thy temple. (125 ad)

Bring Us Nearer

Bring us ever nearer to Thee, O God, that day by day as we come closer to the end of our lives we may be united with the innumerable company of the heavenly host and sing praises to Thee forever. Amen. (109)

Offertory Sentences and Prayer

1. Show yourself in all respects a model of good deeds, and in your teaching show integrity, gravity. *Titus 2:7, R.S.V.*

2. For the needy shall not alway be forgotten, nor the expectation of the poor perish for ever. *Ps. 9:18, A.S.V.*

Almighty God, our Father, by whose will we came into being, and by whose grace we are sustained: With grateful hearts we acknowledge Thy power and Thy love. In token of our appreciation of all Thou hast done for us, we bring these gifts today, praying that Thou wilt bless and use both them and us in Thy service. Through Jesus Christ our Lord. Amen. (91 ad)

33. SUNDAY AFTER ASCENSION DAY (Exaudi)
May 3 to June 6 (Sixth Sunday After Easter)
Color: White

For the Choir

O God: Let Thy grace descend upon us and fill our hearts, that with true reverence we may magnify Thy holy Name. Through Jesus Christ our Lord. Amen. (63)

Opening Sentences

1. The hour cometh, and now is, when the true worshippers shall worship the Father in spirit and in truth: for the Father seeketh such to worship Him. God is a Spirit: and they that worship Him must worship Him in spirit and in truth. *John 4:23, 24.*

2. We have a great High Priest who has passed through the heavens, Jesus, the Son of God. . . . Let us then with confidence draw near to the throne of grace, that we may receive mercy and find grace to help in time of need. *Heb. 4:14, 16, R.S.V.*

Invocation

O Almighty God, Giver of all grace, who pourest out on all who desire it the spirit of grace and supplication: Deliver us, when we draw nigh to Thee, from coldness of heart and wanderings of mind, that with steadfast thoughts and kindled affections we may worship Thee in spirit and in truth. Through Jesus Christ our Lord. Amen. (51 ad)

Scripture Selections (50, 151, 128)

A —	*I Peter*	*4:7–11*	Be Sober and Watch Unto Prayer
	John	*15:26 to 16:7*	The Witness of the Spirit
	(Episcopalians and Lutherans end the Gospel with *v. 4.*)		
O —	*Mark*	*16:14–20*	The Ascension. The Gospel Is Preached
	Luke	*24:50–53*	The Ascension of the Saviour
P —	*Matt.*	*28:16–20*	The Great Commission

General Prayer

Thanks for the Glory of Nature

O God of infinite power: Help us to ascribe to Thee all the glory and honor due to Thy holy Name! Cause us to remember Thy goodness as we see glimpses of Thy greatness in the growth of grass, the beauty of flowers, and the whole work of nature in Thy vast creation. Grant us grace to give glory to Thee also with our lives, that our lives and lips may agree in praise and devotion to Thee. (109)

Help Us to Be Grateful

We thank Thee that Thou didst reveal Thyself in Thy Son. Help us to love Him and enable us to follow Him, to cling to His words, and to be grateful forever for His innocent sufferings and death, His triumphant resurrection, and His glorious ascension, whereby He accomplished our eternal salvation. (109)

For the Church Universal

Almighty and everlasting God, who hast promised to reveal Thy glory through Jesus Christ among all nations: Remember, we beseech Thee, Thy holy Church throughout all the world; unite all who profess and call themselves Christians in the bond of a holy faith as one body, and so replenish them and us with the grace of Thy Holy Spirit, that we may bring forth abundantly the fruits of peace and good works; and that, having persevered in the way of godliness to the end, we may, with prophets, apostles, martyrs, confessors and saints of all ages, come into full communion with Thee and with one another in Thy eternal and glorious Kingdom. (50 ab)

For Home and Kindred

O God, our Heavenly Father, who hast set the solitary in families: Look with favor, we beseech Thee, upon the homes of Thy people. Defend them against all evil, and supply all their needs according to the riches of Thy grace. Make them sanctuaries of purity and peace, love and joy. O Thou Protector and Friend, keep all our dear ones within the safe shelter of Thy love. (46 ab)

Bless Those in Anguish

Bless those who are in any sort of extremity, and answer their prayers according to their several needs. Be with those who are in such anguish that words fail them. Still their minds and hearts. Suffer them not to lose sight of Thee, that they may find strength and comfort in Thy inspiration and power. (109)

Special Intercessions
Guide the World

Guide the destinies of the world, O God, according to Thy holy will. Bestow upon those who ask it the power and the will to relate themselves, their society, and their world according to Thy plan, that the kingdoms of the world may become Thy Kingdom. Through Jesus Christ our Lord. Amen. (109)

Offertory Sentence and Prayer

"He who is faithful in a very little is faithful also in much." *Luke 16:10, R.S.V.*

O God: Accept of Thy infinite goodness these our offerings, and grant that they, being devoted to Thy service, may be used for Thy glory and for the welfare of Thy Church and people. (46) Through Jesus Christ our Lord. Amen.

34. PENTECOST (WHITSUNDAY) (Festival of Pentecost)
May 10 to June 13 (Seven Weeks [50 Days] After Easter)
Color: Red (or White, 147)

Opening Sentences

1. O sing unto the Lord a new song; for He hath done marvelous things: His right hand, and His holy arm, hath gotten Him the victory. The Lord hath made known His salvation: His righteousness hath He openly showed in the sight of the heathen. He hath remembered His mercy and His truth toward the house of Israel: all the ends of the earth have seen the salvation of our God. Make a joyful noise unto the Lord, all the earth: make a loud noise, and rejoice, and sing praise. *Ps. 98:1–4.*

2. "You shall receive power when the Holy Spirit has come upon you; and you shall be My witnesses in Jerusalem and in all Judea and Samaria and to the end of the earth." *Acts 1:8, R.S.V.*

Invocation (or Collect)

O God of the universe, who art nigh unto all who call upon Thee in spirit and truth: Through Thy Holy Spirit inspire and strengthen us who are assembled in this fellowship of prayer, that with Christians of every race and nation we may praise Thy power. For the sake of Jesus Christ our Lord. Amen. (109)

Scripture Selections (50, 157, 151, 128)

A —	*Acts*	*2:1–13*	Pentecost
	John	*14:23–31*	The Outpouring of the Holy Spirit
	(Episcopalians are referred to *Acts 2:1–11* and *John 14:15–31*.)		
E —	*Eph.*	*2:19–22*	Fellow Citizens with the Saints
	John	*14:15–21*	The Gift of the Holy Spirit
	Ezek.	*36:22–28*	God's Promise of a New Spirit
P —	*Acts*	*10:34–48*	Peter Preached and the Holy Spirit Fell on Them That Heard
	John	*3:16–21*	God So Loved the World
	Isa.,	*ch. 61*	The Spirit of the Lord Is Upon Me

General Prayer

THANKS FOR PENTECOST

O God, who didst send the Holy Spirit to enkindle the zeal of Christ's followers in the Early Church: We praise Thee for this manifestation of power; we thank Thee for building Thy Church upon the foundation of the apostles and prophets, Jesus Christ Himself being the chief cornerstone; we rejoice that Thou hast promised the Comforter to Thy people everywhere! (127 and 66)

FOR THE INNER MAN

O Thou blessed Spirit of light and truth: Descend upon all who are assembled in prayer today. Dispel all darkness from our hearts. Spirit of prayer, help us to pray as we ought. Spirit of power, strengthen us in the face of temptations, and work in us both to will and to do according to Thy pleasure. Spirit of holiness, sanctify us in body, mind, and soul, that we may truly follow Him who is the Way, the Truth, and the Life. Be to us all a wall of defense in temptation, a beacon light in the hour of danger, a guide into all truth in times of doubt, and an anchor of hope in moments of despair. (66)

FOR THE UNITY OF GOD'S PEOPLE

O God, the Father of our Lord Jesus Christ, our only Saviour, the Prince of Peace: Give us grace seriously to lay to heart the great dangers we are in by our unhappy divisions. Take away all hatred and prejudice, and whatever else may hinder us from godly union and concord, so that, as there is but one hope of our calling, one Lord, one faith, one baptism, we may be all of one heart and of one soul, united in one holy bond of truth and peace, of faith and love, and may with one mind and one mouth glorify Thee. (126 ad)

FOR MINISTERS

O God, who on the Day of Pentecost didst send down tongues of fire upon the heads of Thy holy apostles, to teach them and lead them into all truth, giving them boldness with fervent zeal to preach the Gospel to all nations: Bless, O Lord, all Thy servants everywhere; give the Holy Spirit to all who teach and all who learn; send forth men and women full of faith and of the Holy Spirit, mighty in the Scriptures, and able ministers of the New Testament. Let Thy ministers be examples to their flock in word, in conversation, in charity, in spirit, in faith, in purity; workmen that need not be ashamed, rightly dividing the word of truth; prepared and willing to endure affliction, to do the work of evangelists, and to make full proof of their ministry; and upon the seed of Thy Word sown by them pour down, O Lord, we beseech Thee, the continual dew of Thy heavenly blessing, that it may take root downward, and bear fruit upward, to Thy honor and glory, and to a joyful ingathering of a spiritual harvest of souls at the great day of harvest, to glorify forever Thy holy Name. (40 ad)

SPECIAL INTERCESSIONS
FOR OUR COUNTRY

O most powerful Lord God, blessed and only Potentate, who hast granted unto our country liberty, and established it in righteousness by the people's will: Guide and direct the multitudes whom Thou hast ordained in power, that their counsels may be filled with knowledge and equity, and the commonwealth be preserved in peace and unity, in strength and honor. Take under Thy protection Thy servants the President, the Governor of this state, the lawgivers, the judges, and all who are entrusted with authority, so defending them from evil and enriching them with good that the people may prosper in freedom beneath an equal law and our nation may advance Thy Kingdom in this world. (129 ad)

COMMUNION OF SAINTS

O God, before whose face the generations rise and pass away, the Strength of those who labor, and the Repose of the blessed dead: We rejoice in the communion of saints. We remember all who have faithfully lived; all who have peacefully died; and especially those most dear to us. Lift us into Thy light and love; and give us at last our portion with those who have trusted in Thee and striven in all things to do Thy holy will. And unto Thy Name, with the Church on earth and the Church in heaven, we ascribe all honor and glory, world without end. Amen. (128)

Offertory Sentence and Prayer

Charge them that are rich in this world, that they be not high-minded, nor trust in uncertain riches, but in the living God, who giveth us richly all things to enjoy; that they do good, that they be rich in good works, ready to distribute, willing to communicate; laying up in store for themselves a good foundation against the time to come, that they may lay hold on eternal life. *I Tim. 6:17-19.*

Dear Father in heaven, who by the power of Thy Holy Spirit dost continue to send Thy servants to go into all the world and preach the Gospel to all nations: Accept our offerings which we present in commemoration of that first great Day of Pentecost. To the end of the earth shall praise, honor, and glory be given to Thee, the Triune God, Father, Son, and Holy Spirit. Amen. (66 ad)

35. TRINITY SUNDAY (Festival of the Holy Trinity)

May 17 to June 20

Color: White

Opening Sentences

1. Holy, holy, holy, is the Lord of Hosts: the whole earth is full of His glory. *Isa. 6:3.*

2. This is the day which the Lord hath made; we will rejoice and be glad in it. *Ps. 118:24.*

Adoration

Glory be to Thee, O Father everlasting, who didst send Thy only-begotten Son into the world, that we might live through Him. Glory be to Thee, O Lord Jesus Christ, who hast brought life and immortality to light through the Gospel. Glory be to Thee, O Holy Spirit, who dost quicken us together with Christ, and dost shed abroad His love in our hearts. Blessed be Thou, Father, Son, and Holy Spirit, one God; and blessed be Thy glorious Name forever. Amen. (128)

Invocation

Almighty and everlasting God, who desirest Thy people to know and confess Thee, the Father, Son, and Holy Spirit, and to worship Thee as the only God in Thy mysterious majesty: Grant, we beseech Thee, that through our holy faith we may be united in living fellowship with Thee. Bless our worship, that we may truly adore Thee, the Triune God, and give Thee praise, glory, and honor forever. Amen. (66 ad)

Scripture Selections (50, 157, 151, 128)

A — *Rom.* *11:33–36*   The Depth of the Riches
    John *3:1–15*   Jesus and Nicodemus
    (Episcopalians are referred to *Rev. 4:1–11.*)

E — *Eph.*	*1:3–14*	Blessed with Spiritual Blessings
Matt.	*28:16–20*	The Great Commission
Isa.	*6:1–8*	Isaiah's Vision of the Lord's Glory
P — *Rev.*	*4:1–11*	Holy, Holy, Holy Is the Lord God Almighty
John	*4:1–26*	The Samaritan Woman. Worship in Spirit

General Prayer

THANKS UNTO THE TRIUNE GOD

O God, who dwellest in the light unapproachable: We render unto Thee most hearty thanks and we praise Thy holy Name for revealing Thyself unto us as Father, Son, and Spirit. We bless Thee, we worship Thee, we give thanks unto Thee, Thou ever glorious and mighty God. Lord God, Heavenly King and Almighty Father; Lord God, Jesus Christ, Thou Lamb of God who takest away the sins of the world; Lord God, Holy Spirit, our Comforter and Guide: Have mercy on us and hear our prayers. (66 ad)

FOR OUR HOMES

O God of all the families of the earth: We pray that purity, love, and honor may dwell in our homes, and duty and affection be the bond of family life; help us to train our children in the ways of reverence and truth; and keep those absent from us under the shield of Thy care. (128 ab)

FOR OUR LAND

Almighty God, who hast given us this good land for our heritage: We beseech Thee that we may always prove ourselves a people mindful of Thy favor and glad to do Thy will. Bless our land with honorable industry, sound learning, and pure manners. Save us from violence, discord, and confusion; from pride and arrogancy; and from every evil way. Defend our liberties, and fashion into one happy people the multitudes brought hither out of many kindreds and tongues. Endue with the spirit of wisdom those to whom in Thy Name we entrust the authority of government, that there may be justice and peace at home, and that, through obedience to Thy law, we may show forth Thy praise among the nations of the earth. (126 ab)

SPECIAL INTERCESSIONS
INTERCESSIONS FOR INDIVIDUALS

O God of mercy, who dost hear our prayers for others: We plead for those who are lonely. Through new associations and activities give them such consolations as may be needful. (109)

We entreat Thee on behalf of those who feel discouraged or disappointed; restore courage, hope, and conviction to them, whereby they may have newness of life. (109)

We implore Thy mercy upon those who bring Thee a sensitive understanding of their unworthiness; give to them such assurance of Thy forgiving love that they may be confident of Thy Fatherly care. (109)

We beseech Thee to comfort those who are ill. By the knowledge that all things work together for the good to those who love Thee, assure them that Thou wilt enable them to await Thy healing with patience; Thy peace with hope; Thy house of many mansions with faith. (109)

We entreat Thee to give strength and power to those who are seriously working for the welfare of their country; but most especially grant Thy Spirit to them, that they may work and labor wisely for the realities which abide. (109)

SUPPLICATIONS

O God, who hast taught us in everything, by prayer and supplication, with thanksgiving, to make our requests known unto Thee: Give ear, we beseech Thee, to our prayer, and hearken to the voice of our supplication. (107)

Enable us to love and trust Thee as our Heavenly Father; to walk in love, as Thy children; and in all things to honor Thy Name and keep Thy commandments. (107)

Make us perfect in Christ Jesus; grant us all to receive of His fullness, and to rest in Him forevermore. (107)

Let the Holy Spirit dwell in us, sanctifying us in spirit and soul and body, and uniting us with all saints in perfect love and eternal joy. (107)

O God, who in the work of man's redemption hast made Thyself known as Father, Son, and Holy Spirit: We beseech Thee to keep us in the faith into which we were baptized; reveal to us the power and riches of Thy grace; and enable us so to glorify Thee in this life that we may enjoy Thy blessed presence in the world to come, and join with angels and archangels in praising Thee, Father, Son, and Holy Spirit. (107 ad)

These things we ask, O Heavenly Father, in patient confidence and joyful hope, being assured that we ask them according to Thy will; that the prayers of Thy Church are heard by Thee; that the intercessions of the Holy Spirit are known to Thee; and that the mediation of Thy well-beloved Son does prevail with Thee. Wherefore we worship and adore Thy glorious Name; ascribing unto Thee, Father, Son, and Holy Spirit, ever one God, all power, might, majesty, and dominion, world without end. Amen. (107 ad)

Offertory Sentences and Prayer

1. Do not be deceived; God is not mocked, for whatever a man sows, that he will also reap. *Gal. 6:7, R.S.V.*

2. David said, "Neither will I offer burnt-offerings unto Jehovah my God which cost me nothing." *II Sam. 24:24, A.S.V.*

Accept these our offerings, O God, we beseech Thee, which now we seek to dedicate to the service of Thy holy Church, and grant us ever to have grateful hearts. Through Jesus Christ our Lord. Amen. (113)

36. FIRST SUNDAY AFTER TRINITY (Second Sunday After Pentecost)

May 24 to June 27
Color: Green; *Lutherans:* White

Opening Sentences

1. O ye servants of the Lord, praise the Name of the Lord. . . .
From the rising of the sun unto the going down of the same the
Lord's Name is to be praised. *Ps. 113:1, 3.*

2. The Lord is righteous in all His ways, and holy in all His
works. The Lord is nigh unto all them that call upon Him, to all
that call upon Him in truth. He will fulfil the desire of them that
fear Him: He also will hear their cry, and will save them. *Ps.
145:17–19.*

Invocation

Almighty God, our Heavenly Father, in whom alone our hearts
find rest and peace: We beseech Thee to reveal Thyself to us in this
hour of worship; pour down upon us Thy spiritual gifts; and grant
that this season of holy quiet may be profitable to us in heavenly
things, and refresh and strengthen us to finish the work Thou hast
given us to do. Through Jesus Christ our Lord. Amen. (46)

Scripture Selections (50, 157)

A — *I John   4:16–21*   God Is Love
    Luke   16:19–31   The Rich Man and Poor Lazarus
    (Episcopalians are referred to *I John 4:7–21* for the Epistle.)

General Prayer

THANKS FOR WORSHIP

Holy, holy, holy, art Thou, O Lord of Hosts; the whole earth is
full of Thy glory. We thank Thee that we may lift up our hearts to
worship Thee in awe and reverence. (66 ad)

Prayer of Confession

Almighty and most merciful Father, who callest the sinner to forsake his way and to return to Thee for mercy: We humbly acknowledge before Thee our manifold sins and shortcomings. We have grievously sinned against Thee in thought, word, and deed. We have broken Thy holy commandments and have departed from Thy ways. We have not fulfilled the law of Christ in bearing one another's burdens. We have not loved our neighbors as ourselves; we have not done to others as we would that they should do to us; we have sought too much our own gain and advantage, and have closed our hearts against our fellow men, forgetting that we are members one of another. Turn us again to Thyself, and suffer us not to fall away from Thee, for Thou dost redeem Thy people from all their iniquities. (45 ad)

For Steadfastness

O God: Speak to our hearts when men faint for fear, and the love of many grows cold, and there is distress in the nations upon earth. Keep us steadfast in the things that cannot be shaken, abounding in hope, and knowing that our labor in Thee is not in vain. Restore our faith in the omnipotence of good; renew the love which never fails; and make us to lift up our eyes to behold the things which are unseen and eternal. (48 ad)

For Kindness

O God of Love, who makest Thy sun to rise on the evil and the good, and sendest rain on the just and the unjust: Grant that we may become more and more Thy true children, by receiving into our souls more of Thy own spirit of ungrudging and unfailing kindness. (76)

For Children

O Lord Jesus Christ, who dost embrace children with the arms of Thy mercy, and dost make them living members of Thy Church: Give them grace, we pray Thee, to stand fast in Thy faith, to obey Thy Word, and to abide in Thy love, that, being made strong by

Thy Holy Spirit, they may resist temptation and overcome evil, and may rejoice in the life that now is and dwell with Thee in the life that is to come. Through Thy merits, O merciful Saviour, who with the Father and the Holy Spirit livest and reignest, one God, world without end. (126 ad)

Special Intercessions
For the Family of Nations

Almighty God, our Heavenly Father: Guide, we beseech Thee, the nations of the world into the way of justice and truth, and establish among them that peace which is the fruit of righteousness, that they may become the Kingdom of our Lord. (126 ab)

A Collect for Love

O God, who hast prepared for those who love Thee such good things as pass man's understanding: Pour into our hearts such love toward Thee, that we, loving Thee above all things, may obtain Thy promises, which exceed all that we can desire. Through Jesus Christ our Lord. Amen. (9 ad)

Offertory Sentence and Prayer

Bring ye all the tithes into the storehouse, that there may be meat in Mine house, and prove Me now herewith, saith the Lord of Hosts, if I will not open you the windows of heaven, and pour you out a blessing, that there shall not be room enough to receive it. *Mal. 3:10.*

Heavenly Father, who hast given us all things richly to enjoy, graciously receive these our gifts as tokens of our gratitude for Thy mercies. Bless them that they may accomplish much good. For Christ's sake. Amen. (113 ad)

37. SECOND SUNDAY AFTER TRINITY (Third Sunday After Pentecost)

May 31 to July 4
Color: Green

Opening Sentences

Great is the Lord, and greatly to be praised; and His greatness is unsearchable. All Thy works shall praise Thee, O Lord; and Thy saints shall bless Thee. *Ps. 145:3, 10.*

Invocation

Almighty and merciful God and Father: Gathered in Thy sanctuary, we call upon Thee to fill us with the spirit of grace and prayer, that we may not only worship Thee with our lips, but draw near with our hearts and worship Thee in spirit and truth. Through Jesus Christ our Lord. Amen. (66 ad)

Scripture Selections (50, 157)

A — *I John*   *3:13–18*   Love in Deed and in Truth
    Luke   *14:16–24*   The Great Supper
    (Episcopalians list *I John 3:13–24* as the Epistle.)

General Prayer

PRAISE FOR FREEDOM OF WORSHIP

Almighty God, who art high and lifted up, and who art blessed, good, gracious, and merciful: We rejoice that we may bow before Thee in adoration and petition, for Thou art ever willing to hear us. Accept our heartfelt thanks for the privilege of worshiping Thee and approaching Thy throne of grace with all our needs. Help us to promote the faithful use of the freedom we have to worship Thee. (109)

FOR BLESSING ON PUBLIC WORSHIP

O Heavenly Father: Forasmuch as none can come to receive Thy holy Word except Thou draw them by Thy gracious inspiration, we beseech Thee to pour out Thy Holy Spirit upon all who worship

Thee today in various places, that their hearts may be inclined favorably to receive, steadfastly to retain, and obediently to perform, whatsoever shall be taught them in Thy Name. (41 ab)

Make the Church Great

We beseech Thee to impart Thy Holy Spirit to the Church throughout the world that it may become an ever greater fellowship of prayer and praise. Make it loyal to Thee in its distinctive task of proclaiming Thy ways to men, women, and children. Suffer it not to lose time and opportunity with trivialities. Awaken Thy people everywhere that they may desire to find in the Church those things which the world can neither give nor take away. (109)

Supply All Our Needs

O God, most holy, wise, and powerful Preserver and Governor of all Thy creatures: Keep us, we beseech Thee, in health of body and soundness of mind, in purity of heart and cheerfulness of spirit, in contentment with our lot and charity with our neighbor, and further all our lawful undertakings with Thy blessing. In our labor strengthen us; in our pleasure purify us; in our difficulties direct us; in our perils defend us; in our troubles comfort us; and supply all our needs according to the riches of Thy grace in Christ Jesus. (127 ab)

Special Intercessions

A Prayer of Saint Chrysostom

Almighty God, who hast given us grace at this time with one accord to make our common supplications unto Thee, and dost promise that where two or three are gathered together in Thy Name Thou wilt grant their requests: Fulfill now, O Lord, the desires and petitions of Thy servants, as may be most expedient for them, granting us in this world knowledge of Thy truth, and in the world to come life everlasting. Amen. (20)

Offertory Sentences and Prayer

1. Be steadfast, immovable, always abounding in the work of the Lord, knowing that in the Lord your labor is not in vain. *I Cor. 15:58, R.S.V.*

2. Bear one another's burdens, and so fulfill the law of Christ. *Gal. 6:2, R.S.V.*

We thank Thee, O Heavenly Father, for the privilege of giving to Thee of that which Thou hast given to us. Help us to understand how to give, as becomes those who receive so richly from Thy bounty. May this offering be wisely spent and carry a blessing with it. We ask it for Thy glory. Amen. (66)

Suggestion

Attention may be given to some of the following Special Days in the summer and fall: Independence Day Sunday (unit 44); Labor Day Sunday (unit 45); World-wide Communion Sunday (unit 46); Missions Sunday (unit 47); Reformation Sunday (unit 48); World Order or World Peace Sunday (unit 49); Thanksgiving (unit 50); Stewardship Sunday (unit 41); Memorial Sunday or All Saints' Day (unit 51); and Universal Bible Sunday (unit 52).

38. THIRD SUNDAY AFTER TRINITY (Fourth Sunday After Pentecost)

June 7 to July 11

Color: Green

Opening Sentences

Praise ye the Lord. Praise God in His sanctuary: . . . Praise Him for His mighty acts: praise Him according to His excellent greatness. Let every thing that hath breath praise the Lord. Praise ye the Lord. *Ps. 150:1, 2, 6.*

Invocation

Eternal God, in whose presence we have met to offer praise: Grant that our ears may be closed to clamor and dispute and open to the voice of Thy songs; that our eyes may behold Thy majesty as well as Thy great love; that our tongues may speak the truth and sing Thy praise; and that our feet, which have brought us into Thy temple, may walk in the region of light. Amen. (19 ad)

Scripture Selections (50, 157, 151)

A — *I Peter*   *5:6-11*   Humble Yourselves Under the Mighty Hand of God

Luke   *15:1-10*   The Parables of the Lost

(Episcopalians begin the Epistle with *v. 5.*)

General Prayer

THANKSGIVING

Almighty and most merciful Father, from whom comes every good and perfect gift: We give Thee praise and hearty thanks for all Thy mercies; for Thy goodness which has created us; Thy bounty which has sustained us; Thy Fatherly discipline which has corrected us; Thy patience which has borne with us; and Thy love which has redeemed us. (45 ad)

We Seek Mercy

Help us to seek Thy throne with penitent hearts that we may receive mercy. Cleanse us from all sins and grant us a consciousness of Thy nearness for all the trials and temptations of our daily pilgrimage. (66 ad)

For Sunday Observance

O Lord of the Sabbath: We rejoice that Thou hast made Sunday for man, when we may set aside our work to adore Thee and study Thy Word. Through worship, relaxation, and a change of activities, help us to gain strength for another week. Inspire everyone who observes this sacred day by remembering Thee in meditation, prayer, and kindly deeds, that they may rejoice daily in Thy Word and power. (109)

For the Church

Give to all professing Christians throughout the world a faith that never slumbers and a love that never fails. Empower us to build the household of faith on the foundation of our Saviour. Inspire all churches to live and move and have their being in Thy great Spirit of love and truth. (109)

For the Sick

Almighty Father, Giver of life and health: Look mercifully, we beseech Thee, on the sick and suffering, especially those for whom our prayers are desired. Let Thy blessing be upon them and upon those who minister unto them. Restore them, if it be Thy gracious will, to health of body and mind, and give them the grace to return and give thanks unto Thee for all Thy benefits. (50 ad)

Special Intercessions
For Humility

O Lord Jesus Christ, Son of Man, who didst come not to be ministered unto but to minister: Give us grace, we beseech Thee, to lay aside the garments of our vanity; and so gird us with Thy power, and crown us with Thy humility, that finally in the glory of servanthood we may stand beside Thy throne, where with the Father and the Holy Spirit Thou reignest, one God, world without end. Amen. (122)

Offertory Sentences and Prayer

1. Do not neglect to do good and to share what you have, for such sacrifices are pleasing to God. *Heb. 13:16, R.S.V.*

2. "No servant can serve two masters; for either he will hate the one and love the other, or he will be devoted to the one and despise the other. You cannot serve God and mammon." *Luke 16:13, R.S.V.*

Most gracious God, who hast made us stewards of Thy bounty, and trusted us with the use of Thy gifts: We lift our hearts in thanksgiving for the many evidences of Thy surrounding love. For all that Thou art to us, and all that we may be to Thee, we give thanks unto Thee, not only with our gifts today, but with our lives throughout the week. Through Jesus Christ our Lord. Amen. (99 ad)

39. LAST SUNDAY IN THE CHURCH YEAR (Sunday Next Before Advent)

November 22 to December 2

Color: Green

Opening Sentences

1. Praise ye the Lord. I will praise the Lord with my whole heart, in the assembly of the upright, and in the congregation. The works of the Lord are great. . . . Holy and reverend is His Name. . . . His praise endureth for ever. *Ps. 111:1, 2, 9, 10.*

2. O magnify the Lord with me, and let us exalt His Name together. *Ps. 34:3.*

Invocation

Lord God of heaven and earth, who hast made the Church Thy dwelling place and hast urged us in Thy Word not to forsake the assembling of ourselves together: Regard us in Thy mercy, we beseech Thee, and send Thy Holy Spirit upon us, that our worship may prepare us to serve and glorify Thee in this world and to rejoice with others who have gone before in Thy eternal Kingdom. Through Jesus Christ our Lord. Amen. (66 ad)

Scripture Selections (50, 157, 151)

A — *I Thess.* 5:1–11 Christ's Second Coming to Judgment
Matt. 25:1–13 The Ten Virgins
(Episcopalians for this Sunday are referred to *John 6:5–14* and *Jer. 23:5–8;* the Gospel looks back over Christ's care for His people while the Epistle looks forward to His reign.)

P — *I Cor.* 1:26–31 Unto Us Who Are Saved the Word of the Cross Is the Power of God

John, ch. 17 The Farewell Prayer

General Prayer

THANKSGIVING

O most loving Father, who desirest that we give thanks for all things: (126) We praise Thee, we glorify Thee, we give thanks to Thee for all Thou art to us. For reason and conscience, for nurture and guidance, and for all the gifts of nature and grace — for these and all other merits, known or unknown, remembered or forgotten, we will give thanks to Thee now and evermore. (117 ad)

THANKS FOR CHRISTIANS

Eternal Father of all the faithful: We rejoice that we are enabled by Thy power to walk in the ways of Jesus Christ as those who have gone before us. We praise Thee that through the spoken word, and the printed page, many witnesses have given expression of Thy truth and majesty. We thank Thee for the heroes of the faith, who have shown by kindly deed and virtuous life what it means to be faithful until death. Accept our undying gratitude that one generation after another has carried the lamp for our feet and the light for our paths. (109)

CONFESSION

Almighty God, who art rich in mercy to all those who call upon Thee: Hear us as we come to Thee, humbly confessing our sins and transgressions and imploring Thy mercy and forgiveness. We have broken Thy holy laws by our deeds and by our words, and by the sinful affections of our hearts. We confess before Thee our disobedience and ingratitude, our pride and willfulness, and our failures and shortcomings toward Thee and toward our fellow men. Have mercy upon us, most merciful Father, and of Thy great goodness grant that we may hereafter serve and please Thee in newness of life. (127 ab)

GENERAL SUPPLICATIONS

O Thou who art strong and mighty: We beseech Thee to make us strong in Thee. Give us strength of body, that we may do our work well and cheerfully, and bear the burdens of others. Give us strength of mind, that we may fearlessly accept Thy truth and faithfully hold to it. Give us strength of heart, that we may love Thee with all our powers, and love our neighbor as ourselves. Increase our faith, that we may trust in Thy promises, and keep fast our hold on Jesus Christ our Saviour. (128 ab)

For Those Who Suffer

Since our sufficiency is of Thee, O God, we beseech Thee to hear our prayers for the sick in body, the distressed in mind, and the anxious in spirit. Through Thy healing powers in nature, and through those who have compassion in their hearts and healing in their hands, continue to bless all who look unto Thee. Assure those who suffer mentally that Thou dost care for them. Calm the spirit of all who are troubled about many things. Bestow upon them that perfect peace which comes from a strong faith. Give a double portion of grace to those who feel the sting of unjust treatment from their round of work and activities, and encourage all to face life's uncertainties without fear. (109)

Special Intercessions
For the Republic

Almighty God, who hast heard the prayers of our fathers, and established a nation in freedom according to the people's will: We implore Thy blessing on the Republic: that Thou wouldst grant us peaceful times and fruitful seasons; that Thou wouldst bless our homes, prosper our industries, and defend us from our enemies; that Thou wouldst govern and protect the President of the United States and all to whom authority is given, the Governor of this state, and all lawmakers and judges; that Thou wouldst unite the hearts of the people to dwell together in peaceful relations; and that Thou wouldst enrich our land with liberty and order, godliness and power, for the good of the world and the glory of Thy Name. (129 ad)

In Memory of Departed Loved Ones

Eternal God, our Heavenly Father: We remember on this solemn occasion our loved ones who have departed this life during the past Church year. Graciously draw near to all afflicted and sorrowing hearts and silence every murmur by the assurance that to those who love Thee all things work together for the good. Help all sorrowing ones to look to that hour when their sorrow shall be turned into joy and all tears shall be wiped away from their eyes. (66 ad)

We thank Thee for Thy abundant consolation for all our griefs. We praise Thee for the blessed Saviour who hath conquered death and glorified the grave, and in whom we have the gift of eternal life. Grant that today, as we stand in spirit beside the graves of the departed, we may more fully realize that we have no continuing city here, but seek one to come. Teach us to look for the blessed hope, even the appearance of our Saviour, that at His Second Coming, to judge the world, we may be found acceptable. (66 and 127)

Receive Us at Last

Since we are strangers and pilgrims on earth, help us by true faith and a godly life to prepare for the life to come, doing the work which Thou hast given us to do while it is day, before the night comes when no man can work. And when our last hour shall come, support us by Thy power, and receive us into Thy everlasting Kingdom. Through Jesus Christ, Thy dear Son, our Lord, who reigneth with Thee and the Holy Spirit, ever one God, in all eternity. Amen. (66 ad)

Offertory Sentence and Prayer

Not every one that saith unto Me, Lord, Lord, shall enter into the Kingdom of Heaven; but he that doeth the will of My Father which is in heaven. *Matt. 7:21.*

O God, most merciful and gracious, of whose bounty we have all received: We beseech Thee to accept this offering of Thy people. Remember in Thy love those who have brought it, and the cause for which it is given, and so follow it with Thy blessing that it may promote peace and good will among men. In the Name of our Lord and Saviour, Jesus Christ. Amen. (127 ab)

Suggestion

Optional worship aids for a full memorial emphasis may be found in unit 51.

40. BROTHERHOOD DAY
Or Race Relations Day

The Sunday nearest to February 22 is suggested for Brotherhood Day, and the Sunday nearest to February 12 for Race Relations Day. (Race Relations Day emphasizes the unity of the human race; Brotherhood Day stresses the spirit that should exist between men of various faiths, with special reference to Christians and Jews.) (149)

Opening Sentences or Calls to Worship

1. God is no respecter of persons: but in every nation he that feareth Him, and worketh righteousness, is accepted with Him. *Acts 10:34, 35.*

2. Be strong and of a good courage; be not afraid, neither be thou dismayed: for the Lord thy God is with thee. *Josh. 1:9.*

Invocation

Almighty God, who art most holy, whose mercy is from everlasting to everlasting and whose strength is perfected in our weakness: Help us now to draw near to Thee, that with mind and heart we may worship Thee. Quench our thirst, which remains despite all earthly springs, and satisfy our hunger. Lift us out of our shadows into Thy light, out of our perplexities into Thy clear truth, and out of our troubles into Thy peace. Through Jesus Christ our Lord. Amen. (76)

Scripture Selections (152, 153, 34)

O —	*Isa.*	56:1–8	Keep Justice
	Mark	3:31–35	Whoever Does the Will of God Is My Brother
	Luke	10:25–37	The Good Samaritan
	Gal.	3:23–29	Neither Jew Nor Greek
	Eph.	4:17–32	Put On the New Man
	I Thess.	4:9–18	As Touching Brotherly Love

General Prayer

THANKSGIVING

O God, Giver of life and of all that makes life good: We lift our hearts to Thee and bless Thy Name for all that Thou art and for all that Thou bestowest upon us. We thank Thee not so much for the things we call ours as for those things which we share with all Thy children — sunshine, wind, rain, and the far horizons. We give Thee thanks, not that Thou hast made life easy, but that Thou givest us strength equal to life's demands. We bless Thee not so much for what little we know, but that under the inspiration of Thy Spirit we can learn what life means. We do not thank Thee for what we are, for we are ashamed to remember our wasted talents, but we thank Thee for what in Thy providence we may be. (99 ad)

ON LINCOLN'S OR WASHINGTON'S BIRTHDAY

Heavenly Father: We thank Thee for the great leaders Thou hast given to our nation. Inspire us to sound the note of gratitude again for their nobility, courage, and unselfish devotion to freedom, justice, and truth. We praise Thy holy Name for all the prophets of liberty, peace, and good will among men. Grant, O Heavenly Father, that their noble example may kindle our hearts with a holy zeal for righteousness and unselfish service. Graciously forbid that the high path they trod should seem impractical for us. (66 ad)

LIVING SACRIFICES

Graciously give ear to our supplications. Breathe upon us the spirit of brotherhood; renew in us a clean heart and sound mind; draw us nearer to Thee in the bonds of love and truth; and consecrate our desire to present ourselves as living sacrifices to Thee. (109)

INCREASE BROTHERHOOD IN EVERY NATION

O God, our Father: Increase in every nation the sense of human brotherhood, true respect for men and women, loyalty in service and charity, happiness in work, and justice in reward; that our homes may be kept safe and pure, that our cities may be renewed in beauty and order, and that all the world may reflect the radiance of Thy throne in heaven. (50 ad)

SPECIAL INTERCESSIONS

FOR RACIAL RECONCILIATION

God of all nations: We pray Thee for all the peoples of Thy earth: for those who are consumed in mutual hatred and bitterness; for those who make bloody war upon their neighbors; for those who oppress and for those who groan under cruelty and subjection; for out-caste tribes, the backward, and the downtrodden; for the ignorant, the wretched, and the enslaved. (75)

We beseech Thee to teach mankind to live together in peace, that no man may exploit the weak and no man hate the strong, and that each race may work out its own destiny. Help us to give the honor we owe to those who are Thy children, whatever their color, their race, or their caste. (75) And unto Thee shall be the glory forever. Amen.

Offertory Sentence and Prayer

Beloved, do not imitate evil but imitate good. He who does good is of God. *III John 11, R.S.V.*

O God, who needest not to be enriched with any gifts that we may bring, yet who lovest the cheerful giver: Receive these our offerings which we present before Thee, and with them ourselves, our souls and our bodies, a living sacrifice, holy and acceptable to Thee. Through Jesus Christ our Lord. Amen. (46)

41. STEWARDSHIP SUNDAY (Kingdom Roll Call)
The Latter Part of November or Early December (Fourth Sunday in Lent)

Opening Sentences

1. Your Father knoweth what things ye have need of, before ye ask Him. . . . But seek ye first the Kingdom of God, and His righteousness; and all these things shall be added unto you. *Matt. 6:8, 33.*

2. For I know the thoughts that I think toward you, saith the Lord, thoughts of peace. . . . Then shall ye call upon Me, and ye shall go and pray unto Me, and I will hearken unto you. And ye shall seek Me, and find Me, when ye shall search for Me with all your heart. *Jer. 29:11–13.*

Invocation

O God, whose Spirit searchest all things, and whose love bears all things: Encourage us to draw near to Thee in sincerity and in truth. Save us from a worship of the lips while our hearts are far away. Save us from attempting to conceal ourselves from Thee, who searchest the heart. (102)

Enable us to acknowledge our dependence on Thy holiness, which seeks to transform our uncleanness; Thy patience, which forgives our unfaithfulness; Thy truth, which reproaches all our falsity and sin. In this worship hour help us to dedicate ourselves to Thee. Amen. (102 ad)

Scripture Selections (141)

O — *Mark*	*12:13–17*	The Tribute Money
Mark	*12:41–44*	The Widow's Mite
Luke	*12:13–21*	The Self-indulgent Fool
Luke	*12:22–34*	Where Your Treasure Is
II Cor.	*9:6–15*	Generosity — Sowing Bountifully

General Prayer

PRAYER OF PRAISE

O God, by whose Word and wisdom we are made partakers of life eternal: We thank Thee for the fresh aids to holy living that every new experience provides and for all Thy stewards, distant or near, who have lived in faith and nobleness of deed; but chiefly we thank Thee for the Light of the World, our Saviour Jesus Christ: for the battle He fought and the victory He won; for His abiding presence in the world He loved; and for the promise that all races and kingdoms shall finally acknowledge Him as Lord and Saviour. (53 ad)

THANKSGIVING

We thank Thee for all the good things of this life: for food, clothing, and shelter; for work to do and zest in the doing of it. We thank Thee for the perpetual touch of the Divine in life, for the image of Thyself in the soul of man; for the vigor of youth, the wisdom of age, and all the lessons of experience; the steps by which we climb to higher things; for the courage of the brave, the indignation of the righteous, the kindness of the thoughtful, and all that keeps us Godlike. (118 ad)

WE ACKNOWLEDGE THY LORDSHIP

We acknowledge Thy Lordship in all things, O God of heaven and earth, who controllest the whole universe, our world and everything in it. Be pleased to accept our gratitude for Thy mastery of life in all its forms. Help us to present ourselves willingly in the service of Thy Son who offered His life for us all. (109)

CONFESSION

For the disciplines that brought no increase in the use of time, talents, and substance for others, and for the rebukes of conscience that led to no amendment of life, have mercy upon us, O God, we humbly entreat Thee. (53 ad)

For the counsels of Thy Word which we have known and not loved, for the Gospel of Thy Son which we have believed and not obeyed, and for the leading of the Spirit of truth which we have acknowledged and not followed, have mercy upon us, O God, we humbly entreat Thee. (53)

Special Intercessions
For the Church

O God: We pray for Thy Church, which is set today amid the perplexities of a changing order, and face to face with a great new task. . . . Baptize her afresh with the life-giving spirit of Jesus. Grant her a new birth, though it be with the travail of repentance and humiliation. Bestow upon her a more imperious responsiveness to duty, a swifter compassion with suffering, and an utter loyalty to the will of God. Put upon her lips the ancient Gospel of her Lord. Help her to proclaim boldly the coming of the Kingdom of God and the doom of all that resist it. Fill her with the prophets' scorn of tyranny, and with a Christlike tenderness for the heavy-laden and downtrodden. Give her faith to espouse the cause of the people, and in their hands that grope after freedom and light to recognize the bleeding hands of the Christ. Bid her cease from seeking her own life, lest she lose it. Make her valiant to give up her life to humanity, that like her crucified Lord she may mount by the path of the cross to a higher glory. (108 ab)

For Loyalty

Almighty God: Grant us the gift of loyalty. For our homes give us love and obedience; for our country, sacrifice and service; for our churches, reverence and devotion; and in everything make us true to Thee. Through Thy Son our Saviour, Jesus Christ our Lord. Amen. (64)

Offertory Sentences and Prayer

1. The earth is the Lord's, and the fulness thereof; the world, and they that dwell therein. *Ps. 24:1.*

2. But thou shalt remember the Lord thy God: for it is He that giveth thee power to get wealth, that He may establish His covenant which He sware unto thy fathers. *Deut. 8:18.*

Almighty God, who from ancient times hast put into the hearts of

Thy people to make offerings for Thy service and the use of Thy house, and who hast been pleased at all times to accept gifts at their hands: We hereby dedicate to Thee and Thy Church these gifts of Thy people. May Thy blessing rest upon them, that Thy Name may be exalted in all the world and that all men everywhere may seek after Thee and find Thee. Through Jesus Christ our Lord. Amen. (75)

42. MOTHER'S DAY (Festival of the Christian Home)
Second Sunday in May

Opening Sentences

1. Surely the Lord is in this place. . . . This is none other but the house of God, and this is the gate of heaven. *Gen. 28:16, 17.*

2. You have come to Mount Zion and to the city of the living God, the heavenly Jerusalem, and to innumerable angels in festal gathering, and to the assembly of the first-born who are enrolled in heaven, and to a Judge who is God of all. . . . Therefore let us be grateful for receiving a Kingdom that cannot be shaken, and thus let us offer to God acceptable worship, with reverence and awe. *Heb. 12:22, 23, 28, R.S.V.*

3. Except the Lord build the house, they labor in vain that build it. *Ps. 127:1.*

4. As for me and my house, we will serve the Lord. *Josh. 24:15.*

Invocation

Most gracious Father, who withholdest no good thing from Thy children and in Thy providence hast brought us to this day of rest and renewal of the soul: Illumine our spirits as we come before Thee in worship. Deliver us from proud thoughts and vain desires, that with lowly hearts we may draw near to Thee and embrace the riches of Thy grace. In the Name and Spirit of Jesus Christ we pray. Amen. (53, 127, 36)

Collect

O God of Love, who didst wonderfully bless the mother and home of our Lord Jesus: Bless the mothers and homes of the world today, that all hearts may be willing to worship Thee and obey Thy commandments. Through Jesus Christ our Lord. Amen. (109)

Scripture Selections (153, 152, 109)

O —	*Gen.*	*29:13–30*	Jacob Marries Leah and Rachel
	Ex.	*1:22 to 2:10*	Moses' Mother

Ruth	1:16, 17	Whither Thou Goest I Will Go
I Sam.	1:4–20	Samuel's Mother in Prayer
Prov.	31:10–31	Description of a Worthy Woman
Mark	10:2–9	Whom God Has Joined Together
Col.	3:12–25	Ideals for Family Life
I Tim.	5:1–10	Honor Widows — Duties of Widows
II Tim.	1:1–6, 13, 14	Timothy's Home
Titus	2:1–10	Qualities of a Christian Home

General Prayer

THANKSGIVING

With our whole heart we give Thee thanks, most gracious Father, for the world in which we now struggle, suffer, and aspire; for that better world of final achievement for which we hope; for the mercy that is new every morning, fresh every evening, and as varied as our ever-changing needs; for the gifts of faith and hope which make perpetual sunshine within us and around; for the tenderness of Thy compassion in every time of our discomfort; for Thy preserving mercy through all the days of our life; for the protection and comfort of our homes; and for all who love us and whom we love. (53 and 142)

FOR MOTHERS AND GIRLS

O God: We offer Thee praise and benediction for the sweet ministries of motherhood in human life. We bless Thee for our own dear mothers who built up our lives by theirs; who bore us in travail and loved us the more for the pain we gave; who nourished us at the breast and hushed us to sleep in the warm security of their arms. We thank Thee for their tireless love, for their voiceless prayers, for the agony with which they followed us through our sins and won us back; for the Christly power of sacrifice and redemption in mother-love. We pray Thee to forgive us if in thoughtless selfishness we have taken their love as our due without giving the tenderness which they craved as their sole reward. And if the great treasure of a mother's life is still spared to us, may we do for her feebleness what she did for ours. (108)

Put upon the girls of our people the awe of their future calling, that they may preserve their bodies and minds in purity and strength for the holy task to which the future may summon them. (108 ab)

For Family Altars

Through the altar of worship in the home, and whatever other means Thou dost employ, we beseech Thee to hallow and sweeten the fellowship in our homes, shielding us from temptation, comforting us in our sorrows, and strengthening us for helpfulness. Quicken our religious life and tighten the cords that bind the members of our families to Thee and to things heavenly and eternal. (66 ad)

For the Absent

O Lord, our God, who art in every place, from whom we can be separated by no space or distance: Keep all dear ones from whom we are now separated, and grant that both they and we, by drawing nearer to Thee, may be drawn nearer to each other, bound together by the unseen chain of Thy love. (87)

Special Intercessions
For the Sick and Others

O God, whose blessed Son healed all manner of sickness and disease among the people: Continue His gracious work in the homes and hospitals of our land. Grant that all physicians, surgeons, and nurses may have the mind that was in Christ Jesus, and receive Thy heavenly aid in their ministrations. (107)

Comfort and sustain those who are in trouble, whether of body, mind, or estate. Defend the weak, the needy, the afflicted, the widowed, and the fatherless. (107)

Most gracious God: We beseech Thee for all who are near and dear to us; for little children, that they may be kept in their innocence; for aged folk, that they may enjoy the best of life at eventide; for men busy with the affairs of life, and women burdened with household cares, that the peace which Thou alone canst give may fill their hearts and minds. (142 ad)

A Final Supplication

O Thou who art the Light of the minds that know Thee, the Life of the souls that love Thee, and the Strength of the hearts that seek Thee: Help us so to know Thee that we may truly love Thee; so to love Thee that we may fully serve Thee; and so to serve Thee that we may sincerely seek to glorify Thee. Through Jesus Christ our Lord. Amen. (9 and 109)

Offertory Sentence and Prayer

Every man shall give as he is able, according to the blessing of the Lord. *Deut. 16:17.*

Unto Thee, O Lord, do we offer the gift of our hands and the loyalty of our hearts. Accept us, with our gifts, we pray, in Jesus' Name. Amen. (82)

43. MEMORIAL DAY SUNDAY

May 30 or the Sunday Before

Opening Sentences

1. Great is the Lord, and greatly to be praised in the city of our God, in the mountain of His holiness. . . . This God is our God for ever and ever: He will be our Guide even unto death. *Ps. 48:1, 14.*

2. The righteous shall be had in everlasting remembrance. *Ps. 112:6, A.S.V.*

3. Let us now praise famous men, and our fathers that begat us. The Lord manifested in them great glory, . . . and their name liveth to all generations. *Ecclesiasticus 44:1, 2, 14.*

4. The righteous live for ever, and in the Lord is their reward, and the care for them with the Most High. Therefore shall they receive the crown of royal dignity and the diadem of beauty from the Lord's hand. *Wisdom of Solomon 5:15, 16.*

Invocation

O God, who art, and wast, and art to come, before whose face the generations rise and pass away: Be to us a cloud by day and a fire by night. O Thou sole Source of peace and righteousness, take now the veil from every heart, and join us in one fellowship with Thy prophets and saints who have trusted in Thee; and in this hour of devotion accept our humble worship of Thy great Name. Through Jesus Christ our Lord. Amen. (88 ad)

Scripture Selections (109, 128)

O — *Josh.*	*4:4–8, 21–24*	What Do You Mean by These Stones?
II Sam.	*23:8–23*	The Names of David's Mighty Men
Ps.	*145*	I Will Extol Thee, My God, O King
Isa.	*43:1–21*	Fear Not, for I Have Redeemed Thee
Heb.	*11:1 to 12:2*	The Triumphs of Faith Set Forth

P — *Rev.*	7:9-17	A Great Multitude Before the Lamb
John	14:1-15	Let Not Your Heart Be Troubled
Ps.	46	God, the Refuge of His People

General Prayer

THANKS FOR PAST SACRIFICES

O Lord our God, in whose hands are the living and the dead: As we approach Thy throne in this memorial service, we give Thee thanks for all who have laid down their lives in the service of our country. We thank Thee for their heroism and self-sacrifice. Above all we thank Thee for the great Captain of our salvation, Christ our Lord, who laid down His life that we might live forever. Grant that through His great sacrifice all nations, kindred, and people may be united in a true brotherhood. (66 and 48)

DEDICATION OF MEMORIAL DAY

We thank Thee for those dear to us, forgotten by the world but still living in our hearts, who rest from their labors. Make this day of memory a day of peace and dedication. Bid us further every cause of righteousness and truth. (99 ad)

BLESS AMERICA

We pray, O Lord, that the flag of this nation may ever be an emblem of liberty, justice, and truth. May its white speak to us of purity, its red of courage, and its blue of the eternal home beyond the stars. Bless America. Mercifully protect us, O God, from civil strife and the jealousies of race and class. Purge the land from its evils, and fill it with the Spirit of Christ. Grant peace, prosperity, and happiness to us all, and above all grant that our land may become more and more a righteous nation. (66 ad)

FOR VETERANS OF THE LAST WAR

O God of the far-flung battle lines and the God of universal peace: We implore Thy favor to rest upon the veterans among us from the most recent wars. Help them, we pray Thee, to feel that Thou art as near now as during the roar of planes and the whistle of bombs. Inspire them and all of us with the challenge of a great offensive against all that is wrong and wicked, and help us to employ our strength against every form of evil. (109)

SPECIAL INTERCESSIONS
FOR THE BEREAVED

O Thou who art the God of all comfort, who healest the broken in heart and bindest up their wounds: Mercifully look upon those who are bereaved. Be near to them in their sorrow; draw them nearer to Thee. Grant that the things unseen and eternal may become more full of meaning and power. Sustain them in their sorrow. Stay their minds on Thee in perfect trust. And give them grace to return to their homes and work and to discharge their duties with fidelity and loyalty. (56 ad)

COMMUNION OF SAINTS

O Lord of all worlds, before whom stand the spirits of the living and the dead: We bless Thy holy Name for all Thy servants who have finished their course and kept the faith, and who are now at rest with Thee. Grant us grace to follow their good example, that we with them may finally be partakers of Thy heavenly Kingdom. Take now the veil from every heart, and unite us in one communion with all the saints on earth and the saints in heaven. Through Jesus Christ our Lord, to whom with Thee and the Holy Spirit we ascribe glory in the Church throughout all ages, world without end. Amen. (128)

Offertory Sentence and Prayer

"For whoever would save his life will lose it; and whoever loses his life for My sake and the Gospel's will save it." *Mark 8:35, R.S.V.*

O God, who dost bid us to work while it is day, before the night comes when no man can work: Accept these gifts which we offer in grateful memory of the supreme sacrifice of Thy Son. Help us to lay up treasures for ourselves in heaven. In Jesus' Name. Amen. (109)

44. INDEPENDENCE DAY SUNDAY

July 4 or the Sunday Before (Adaptable for Another National Holiday)

Color: White (158)

Salute to the American Flag

I pledge allegiance to the flag of the United States of America and to the Republic for which it stands: one nation indivisible, with liberty and justice for all. (98)

Salute to the Christian Flag

I pledge allegiance to the Christian flag and to the Saviour for whose Kingdom it stands: one brotherhood, uniting all mankind in service and love. (98)

Opening Sentences

1. Blessed is the nation whose God is the Lord; and the people whom He hath chosen for His own inheritance. *Ps. 33:12.*

2. Ye shall know the truth, and the truth shall make you free. . . . If the Son therefore shall make you free, ye shall be free indeed. *John 8:32, 36.*

3. For freedom Christ has set us free; stand fast therefore, and do not submit again to a yoke of slavery. *Gal. 5:1, R.S.V.*

Invocation

Almighty God, who didst bless us with religious and civil liberty: We thank Thee for all the privileges Thou hast so abundantly bestowed upon us. Help us, and all others who seek Thy favor, to be mindful of Thy many blessings. Stir up, we beseech Thee, such love for Thee that we may be strengthened to serve Thee. And we shall give praise and honor to Thee, world without end. Through Jesus Christ our Lord. Amen. (66 ad, 109)

Scripture Selections (153, 152)

O —	Deut.	4:32–40	Know that the Lord Is God
	Deut.	10:12–15; 11:1–9	What the Lord Requires
	Deut.	30:15–20	I Command Thee to Love the Lord
	Ps.	33	Blessed Is the Nation Whose God Is the Lord
	Ps.	67	Let the Nations Be Glad
	Micah	4:1–5	And He Shall Rebuke Strong Nations
	Matt.	22:15–22	The Things That Are Caesar's and the Things That Are God's
	I Peter	2:9–25	You Are a Royal Priesthood, a Holy Nation

General Prayer

THANKS FOR OUR NATION

Almighty God, who in Thy providence hast made us citizens of a land filled with treasures, opportunities, and privileges: We thank Thee for our ideals of liberty and faith; for the pioneers and fearless leaders who transformed the wilderness into a nation and won for us free institutions; and for all who in government, school, church, homes, in places of business, industry, and on the farm, have sought to make us as a nation an instrument of Thy service. (99 ad)

PRAYER FOR HUMILITY

As a nation, O God, forgive our sins. Pardon our lawlessness, materialism, racial hatred, and all class selfishness. Save us from too much dependence upon temporal things, and set our hearts on the riches of eternity. Give us, we pray Thee, the grace of humility and create a right spirit within us. (90 ad)

FOR OUR RESPONSIBILITIES

Heavenly Father: We pray that as we are made mindful of our privileges and blessings upon this occasion we may also become more and more conscious of our responsibilities. Help us to be true to the great ideals for which our founding fathers stood, that our country may really be the home of justice, liberty, and true brotherhood. Help us to do our duties toward others as before Thee. Give us the courage which our times demand, that we may build a world that will be safe for our children and our children's children. Deliver us from every influence that would break down reverence for law and corrupt our sense of responsibility. Keep alive among us a vital faith in the things of the spirit, a love that makes for beauty and truth, and a devotion to Thy ways of righteousness and peace. (66, 44, 99)

For Those in Authority

O Lord, our Heavenly Father, the high and mighty Ruler of the universe, who dost from Thy throne behold all citizens upon earth: Most heartily we beseech Thee with Thy favor to behold and bless the President of the United States and all others in authority; so replenish them with the grace of Thy Holy Spirit that they may always seek Thy will and walk in Thy way. Defend them from all evil and enrich them with all needed good, that the people may prosper in freedom beneath an equal law, and our nation may magnify Thy Name in all the earth. (66 and 127)

Special Intercessions
For Health and Strength

Almighty God, who art the Source of health and healing, of power and of peace: Grant to us, Thy children, such a consciousness of Thy indwelling presence as may give us strong confidence in Thee. In all pain and weariness and anxiety inspire us to cast ourselves on Thy care, that knowing ourselves fenced about by Thy loving power, we may find in Thee health, strength, and peace. (48 ab)

For these blessings, individual and national, we pray in the Name of Jesus Christ our Lord. Amen. (109)

Offertory Sentence and Prayer

"Render therefore to Caesar the things that are Caesar's, and to God the things that are God's." *Matt. 22:21, R.S.V.*

Almighty God, to whom we present an offering as a token of gratitude for benefits freely given to us: Consecrate these gifts and bless their use. Through Jesus Christ our Lord. Amen. (109)

45. LABOR DAY SUNDAY
Sunday Before Labor Day

For the Choir
Grant, O Lord, that what we will sing with our lips we may believe in our hearts and practice in our lives; that being doers of Thy Word and not hearers only, we may obtain everlasting life. Through Jesus Christ our Lord. Amen. (48 ad)

Opening Sentences
1. Be steadfast, immovable, always abounding in the work of the Lord, knowing that in the Lord your labor is not in vain. *I Cor. 15:58, R.S.V.*
2. Wherewith shall I come before the Lord, and bow myself before the high God? . . . He hath showed thee, O man, what is good; and what doth the Lord require of thee, but to do justly, and to love mercy, and to walk humbly with thy God? *Micah 6:6, 8.*

Invocation
Almighty and most merciful God, who hast appointed to us a portion of labor that we may serve while it is day: We beseech Thee to draw our hearts unto Thy dear Son, that we may receive the rest promised to the heavy-laden; and being forgiven by His mercy, comforted by His Word, refreshed by His Spirit, and lifted by His fellowship, may we find in this hour of worship a blessing for our souls. Through Jesus Christ our Lord. Amen. (127 ad)

Scripture Selections (158, 117)

O — *Ex.*	*3:1–10*	I Have Seen the Oppressions in Egypt
Deut.,	*ch. 8*	Man Does Not Live by Bread Alone
Eccl.	*5:12, 18–20*	The Blessing of Labor
Matt.	*20:1–16*	Laborers in the Vineyard

Mark	*6:1-4*	Is Not This the Carpenter, the Son of Mary?
1 Cor.	*3:6-17*	Fellow Workmen with God
1 Tim.	*6:1-12*	The Secret of Contentment
James	*5:1-6*	Oppressions of the Rich

General Prayer

ADORATION

O God, eternal and unchangeable, the same yesterday, today, and forever; who art glorious in holiness, abundant in grace and truth, and full of love and compassion: Hearken to the praise of Thy people in all places of Thy dominion. We bless Thee for Thy Son, who hath glorified Thee upon earth. We bow down and adore Thee! (50 ad)

FOR THE SPIRIT TO WORK

O Lord, our Heavenly Father, by whose providence the duties of men are varied and ordered: Grant to us all the spirit to labor heartily to do our work in our several stations, in serving one Master and looking for one reward. Teach us to put to good account whatever talents Thou hast given us, and enable us to redeem our time by patience and zeal. (128 ab)

FOR SOCIAL RIGHTEOUSNESS

O God, who hast made us a royal priesthood that we might offer unto Thee prayer and intercession for all sorts and conditions of men: Hear us as we pray: (97)

For all who toil in the burden and the heat of the day, that they may enjoy the rewards of their industry, that they may not be defrauded of their due; (97 ab)

For those who have authority and power over their fellow men, that they may not use it for selfish advantage but be guided to do justice and to love mercy; (97)

For those who have been worsted in the battles of life, whether by the inhumanity of their fellows, their own limitations, or the fickleness of fortune, that they may contend against injustice without bitterness, overcome their own weakness with diligence, and learn how to accept what cannot be altered, with patience; (97)

For the rulers of nations, that they may act wisely and without pride, and seek to promote peace among the peoples and establish justice in our common life; (97)

For the teachers and ministers of the Word, for artists and interpreters of our spiritual life, that they may rightly divide the word of truth and not be tempted by pride or greed or any ignoble passion to corrupt the truth to which they are committed; (97)

For prophets and seers and saints, who awaken us from our sloth, that they may continue to hold their torches high in a world darkened by prejudice and sin and never be disobedient to the heavenly vision. (97)

O God, who hast bound us together in this bundle of life: Give us the grace to understand how our lives depend upon the courage, the industry, the honesty, and the integrity of our fellow men, that we may be mindful of their needs, grateful for their faithfulness, and faithful in our responsibilities to them. (97 ab)

Bless Labor Day

Heavenly Father: Graciously bless Labor Day. Grant an abundant measure of grace that rich and poor, capital and labor, may work together in friendship and fellowship, and confer with one another for the common good. Quicken in the souls of all a deep and abiding sense of our common brotherhood and strengthen the bonds that make us one. (66 ad)

For Christian Workers

Graciously hear our intercessions for those who are without conscious knowledge of Thy love and care. Through Thy Holy Spirit attend the efforts of Thy people who try to follow Thee, that Thy love in their hearts may not lose its power. Restore hope in those who have become disappointed and discouraged in achieving results for Thy cause. Give new inspiration and patience to Thy workers that they may continue the fight of faith in the conquest of evil. (109)

For Students and Teachers

O God of wisdom: Grant to all who are about to enter halls of learning the blessing of knowledge and good fellowship. Strengthen their desire to prepare themselves for the future. Look favorably upon all students and teachers, and guide them that they may grow in understanding. (109)

For Those in Sickness

Heavenly Father, who art touched with the feeling of our infirmities, and dost minister to every need: Grant Thy blessing to those whose strength is turned into weakness because illness has come to them. Help them to be conscious of Thy presence, that they may rest patiently and hopefully in Thy love. Renew their strength, and bring them back to their accustomed duties. And cheer them with the thought that in the realm of the spirit toward which we journey there shall be no more sickness or pain, but everlasting and abundant life. (48)

Special Intercessions

For Final Reward

Help us to look for eternal salvation in Thy Son Jesus Christ, who though He was rich, yet for our sakes became poor, that both poor and rich might have life in Him. Keep our hope and trust in Thee. Enable us to labor faithfully while it is day, before the night comes when no man can work. Receive us at last, and grant us the reward of life through Christ our Lord. In His Name we ask it. Amen. (66 ad)

Offertory Sentence and Prayer

" Take heed, and beware of all covetousness; for a man's life does not consist in the abundance of his possessions." *Luke 12:15, R.S.V.*

Eternal God, who alone abidest while all Thy creatures and material possessions change and pass away: Receive, we pray Thee, these our offerings which we render for the service of Thy Church and its extension, and accept with them our hearts and lives which we consecrate anew to Thee. Through Jesus Christ our Lord. Amen. (53 and 113)

46. WORLD–WIDE COMMUNION SUNDAY
First Sunday in October

For the Choir
We lift our hearts to Thee in gratitude, O Lord, for the privilege of serving in the ministry of music. We remember the power of music to stimulate faith and hope and love. We thank Thee for the influence of song to soothe the troubled, inspire the indifferent, and give fresh heart to the discouraged. Use our voices, we beseech Thee, in the service of the sanctuary. Grant that our lips may be filled with messages from Thee. We ask in the Master's Name. Amen. (72)

Opening Sentences
1. Oh that men would praise the Lord for His goodness, and for His wonderful works to the children of men! For He satisfieth the longing soul, and filleth the hungry soul with goodness. *Ps. 107:8, 9.*

2. "Behold, I stand at the door and knock; if any one hears My voice and opens the door, I will come in to him and eat with him, and he with Me." *Rev. 3:20, R.S.V.*

Invocation (or Collect)
Almighty God, unto whom all hearts are open, all desires known, and from whom no secrets are hid: Cleanse the thoughts of our hearts by the inspiration of Thy Holy Spirit, that we may perfectly love Thee, and worthily magnify Thy holy Name. Through Jesus Christ our Lord. Amen. (11)

Scripture Selections (155 ab)

O — *II Chron.*	*30:5–20*	Pardon for Everyone That Prepares His Heart
Ps.	*32*	Blessed Is He Whose Transgression Is Forgiven
Isa.	*1:10–20*	Though Your Sins Be as Scarlet
Ezek.	*18:21–32*	A New Heart and a New Spirit

Ezek.	33:1–20	When the Wicked Turn from Their Way
Matt.	26:26–29	Drink Ye All of It
John	17:18–23	That They All May Be One
I Cor.	11:17–32	The New Testament in the Blood
Heb.	10:1–17	No More Memory of Past Sins
I John	1:3–9	The Basis of Fellowship
I John	4:16–21	God Is Love

General Prayer

Remembering His Life and Death

Gracious Father, who didst send forth Thy Son our Lord to speak Thy will for man in a life of love and self-sacrifice: We thank Thee for His sympathy with the multitude who hungered for the bread of life and wandered as sheep without a shepherd; for His boundless compassion; for His agony in the Garden; for His acceptance of Thy holy will; for His prayer for those who ignorantly slew Him; for His confidence that at last all evil will be destroyed; and for His return to Thee to be our everlasting Friend and Saviour. (53 ad)

Thanks for His Influence

We remember also and give thanks for the immortal longings which He quickened in the souls of men; for His promise of new heavens and a new earth; for His mild and tolerant spirit; for the guiding lights He kindled; for the works that His servants, sustained by Him, have wrought; for the comfort He hath brought to our souls; and for the confidence with which in His company we face the unknown journey that yet remains. (53 ad)

Prepare Us for Holy Communion

O Lord Jesus Christ, who in a wonderful Sacrament didst leave Thy Church a memorial of Thyself, as a pledge and seal of Thy redeeming love: Grant that when, in obedience to Thy command, we keep the feast, we may approach Thy table with love and humble hope; that, discerning its sacred mystery, we may feed by faith on Thy body and blood, and be made partakers of Thy heavenly grace. Let the remembrance of Thy Passion and triumph ever abide within

our hearts, that we may be fortified against the assaults of our enemies, and strengthened to keep Thy commandments all the days of
our life. (107 ad)

For Righteousness

O God, who puttest into our hearts such deep desires that we cannot be at peace until we rest in Thee: Mercifully grant that the longing of our souls may not go unsatisfied because of any unrighteousness of life that may separate us from Thee. Open our minds to the
counsels of Thy eternal wisdom; breathe into our souls the peace
that passes understanding. Let our hunger and thirst be for righteousness, that we may be filled with the bread of heaven. O Lord,
give us grace to seek first Thy Kingdom; and we know Thou wilt
add all things needful. (117)

For Our Church Organizations

O God, who art pleased when we love Thee with heart, mind, and
strength: We beseech Thee to deepen the desire of organizations and
committees in our church to make progress; grant new life and spirit
to them. Through these and other channels help us to serve Thee
and our fellow men with all our beings, that we may be ever more
effective in the tasks we are trying to do for Thy sake. (109)

For Those Who Are Sick

O Father of mercies and God of all comfort, our only help in time
of need: We humbly beseech Thee to behold, visit, and relieve those
who are sick. Look upon them in Thy mercy; comfort them with
a sense of Thy goodness; and give them patience under their affliction. In Thy good time restore them to health, and enable them to
lead their lives to Thy glory; and grant that they may dwell with
Thee in eternal life. (48 ad)

Special Intercessions
For Christian Unity

O God of peace, who through Thy Son Jesus Christ didst send
forth one faith for the salvation of mankind: Send Thy grace and
heavenly blessing upon all Christian people around the world who

are striving to draw nearer to Thee, and to each other, in the unity of the Spirit and in the bond of peace. Give us penitence for our divisions, wisdom to know Thy truth, courage to do Thy will, love that will break down the barriers of pride and prejudice, and an unswerving loyalty to Thy holy Name. (86)

Suffer us not to shrink from any endeavor that is in accordance with Thy will, for the peace and unity of Thy Church. Give us boldness to seek only Thy glory and Kingdom. Unite us all in Thee as Thou, O Father, with Thy Son and the Holy Spirit, art one God, throughout all ages. Amen. (86 ad)

Offertory Sentences and Prayer

1. " Give, and it will be given to you; good measure, pressed down, shaken together, running over, will be put into your lap. For the measure you give will be the measure you get back." *Luke 6:38, R.S.V.*

2. " The Holy Supper is kept, indeed,
   In whatso we share with another's need;
   Not what we give, but what we share,
   For the gift without the giver is bare;
   Who gives himself with his alms feeds three —
   Himself, his hungering neighbor, and Me." (84)

O Giver of every good and perfect gift: We acknowledge Thy bounty in these gifts which we now offer and dedicate unto Thee. We pray Thee to accept them and multiply them for the work of Thy Church. Through Jesus Christ our Lord. Amen. (116 ab)

Prayer After Communion

Strengthen, O Lord, the hands that have been held out to receive Thy holy things, that they may ever serve Thee. Grant that the tongues that have uttered the " Holy, Holy, Holy," may speak the truth; that the eyes that have seen Thy great love may also behold Thy blessed hope; that the feet that have trod Thy house may walk in the region of light; and that we who have received the living body and blood of Jesus Christ may be restored with newness of life. Through the same Thy Son Jesus Christ our Lord. Amen. (19)

47. MISSIONS SUNDAY

Opening Sentences

1. Blessed be the Lord God, the God of Israel, who only doeth wondrous things. And blessed be His glorious Name for ever: and let the whole earth be filled with His glory. Amen, and Amen. *Ps. 72:18, 19.*

2. And He said unto them, Go ye into all the world, and preach the Gospel to every creature. *Mark 16:15.*

Invocation

Most gracious and merciful God: Vouchsafe unto us who are here assembled in Thy house the joy and the comfort of Thy presence. Show unto us the beauty of holiness, and reveal to us the height and extent of Thy love, that we may come before Thee with childlike confidence, and worship Thee with loving hearts. Through Jesus Christ our Lord and Saviour. Amen. (63 ad)

Scripture Selections (151, 154)

T — *Acts*	*13:44–49*	The Boldness of Paul and Barnabas
Acts	*16:8–10*	Paul's Vision of the Man of Macedonia
Matt.	*9:35–38*	The Harvest Is Plenteous
Ps.	*69*	God Will Save Zion
S — *Acts*	*16:9–15*	Paul's Vision of the Man of Macedonia
Matt.	*9:35–38*	The Harvest Truly Is Plenteous
Matt.	*5:13–16*	Let Your Light Shine Before Men
Zeph.	*3:8–17*	Restoration of Israel
F. S. and O — *Ps.*	*98*	All the Ends of the Earth Have Seen the Salvation
Isa.	*43:1–11*	God Will Gather His Church
Jer.	*9:23–26*	Let Him That Glorieth Glory in Knowing the Lord

Jonah	4:1–11	Jonah and the Gourd
Acts	11:19–26	Spread of the Gospel
Col.	1:2–6	The Gospel in All the World Bringeth Fruit

General Prayer

ADORATION

Holy, Holy, Holy! Lord God Almighty, who hast set Thy glory above the heavens: Hearken to the adoration of Thy people, we beseech Thee, and let the words of our mouths and the meditations of our hearts be acceptable in Thy sight, O Lord, our Strength and our Redeemer. (50 ad)

THANKS FOR THE GOSPEL

We thank Thee, most glorious God, that the witnesses of the cross did not remain in Palestine, but were pleased to speak of Thy glory to people of other countries. We thank Thee for making it possible for us to be partakers of Thy precious Gospel and the Christian heritage. Give us the grace to continue in the work of sharing the news graciously brought to us. (109)

BLESS OUR MISSIONS AT HOME AND ABROAD

Graciously hear us as we pray for all associations and societies engaged in Thy work. Bless the preaching of Thy Word in all Christian congregations and communities, at home and abroad, and pour out Thy Holy Spirit upon those who teach and those who hear. Have mercy on the multitudes of people in our country and elsewhere who blindly pursue their way. Grant them the light of Thy Gospel; open their eyes to see the miracle of Thy grace; empower Thy Church to help them to find light and salvation in Thy Son Jesus Christ. (66 ad)

BLESS OUR MISSIONARIES

Bless all missionaries and other workers in their labors, especially in _____, and in the homeland. Endow them with faith and love, with courage and humility, with wisdom and faithfulness to proclaim the glad tidings with conviction and sincerity, through the power of Thy Holy Spirit. With the might of Thy arms encompass Thy messengers who often stand as sheep in the midst of wolves. Grant unto them health and strength in body and soul. Multiply the number of such who cheerfully engage in Thy service as missionaries. (66 ad)

For Peace

Almighty God, from whom all thoughts of truth and peace proceed: Kindle, we pray Thee, in the hearts of all men the true love of peace, and guide with Thy pure and peaceable wisdom those who take counsel for the nations of the earth; that in tranquillity Thy Kingdom may go forward, until the earth be filled with the knowledge of Thy love. (128 ab)

For the Kingdom

O Father of men, who hast promised that the kingdoms of this world shall become the Kingdom of Thy Son: Purge the nations of error and corruption; overthrow the power of sin; and establish His Kingdom of grace in every land. Incline the hearts of all governors and peoples to the Lord of Lords and the King of Kings, that He may enter into their cities, churches, and homes, to dwell there, and rule all things by His Word and Spirit. (85)

Special Intercessions
Help Us to Labor

Draw near to us in Thy loving-kindness that we may recognize more perfectly the needs of our brethren who are yet far from Thee. Grant unto us abundant grace that we may stand ready, every one according to the gift he has received, to labor in love for the march of faith. Enable us gladly and cheerfully to participate in the task of proclaiming Thy Word across the nation and around the globe. (66 and 109)

Direct us, O Lord, in all our doings with Thy most gracious favor, and further us with Thy continual help; that in all our works, begun, continued, and ended in Thee, we may glorify Thy holy Name, and finally, by Thy mercy, obtain everlasting life. Through Jesus Christ our Lord. Amen. (11, as ad in 126)

Offertory Sentences and Prayer

1. And the Lord spake unto Moses, saying, Speak unto the Children of Israel, that they bring Me an offering: of every man that giveth it willingly with his heart ye shall take My offering. *Ex. 25:1, 2.*

2. Cast thy bread upon the waters: for thou shalt find it after many days. *Eccl. 11:1.*

3. "He who is not with Me is against Me, and he who does not gather with Me scatters." *Matt. 12:30, R.S.V.*

O God of all blessing: We thank Thee for the privilege of sharing in the task of bringing our neighbors near and far to know and love Thee. To assist this work we bring an offering with grateful hearts. Teach us to give cheerfully at all times, since Thou lovest a cheerful giver. Bless the offering as it is sent forth in Thy Name and for Thy sake. Amen. (31 ad)

Suggestion

Other missionary prayers, as in units 10 and 9, may be offered.

48. REFORMATION SUNDAY (Festival of the Reformation)

October 31, or the Sunday before; or the Sunday after, if October 31 falls on a Saturday.

Color: Red (Lutherans list red also for the Sunday after Reformation Sunday)

For the Choir

O God, who art a tower of strength to Thy people: Grant that in the service of Thy temple we may always have thoughts and desires that are pleasing in Thy sight, that everything we sing or say may support Thy holy will and uphold Thy glory. In the Name of Him who came to set us free. Amen. (109)

Opening Sentences

1. He that dwelleth in the secret place of the Most High shall abide under the shadow of the Almighty. I will say of the Lord, He is my Refuge and my Fortress: my God; in Him will I trust. *Ps. 91:1, 2.*

2. Trust in Him at all times; ye people, pour out your heart before Him: God is a Refuge for us. *Ps. 62:8.*

Invocation

Almighty and merciful God, who art our Refuge and Strength: We come before Thee with praise and thanksgiving on this anniversary of the Reformation. Send forth Thy light and Thy truth, we beseech Thee, and bring us to Thy presence, that, beholding Thy glory, we may magnify Thy great and holy Name and be true to Thee till death. Through Jesus Christ our Lord. Amen. (66 and 124)

Scripture Selections (50, 57, 151)

A — *John*	*8:31–36*	The Truth Shall Make You Free
Gal.	*2:16–21*	Christ Lives in Me

E — *I Cor.*   *3:11-23*   Christ the Only Foundation for Life and
                           Salvation
  John   *2:13-17*   Jesus Cleanses the Temple
  Ps.   *46*   God Is Our Refuge and Strength

General Prayer

THANKS FOR THE REFORMATION

Eternal God and Heavenly Father, God of infinite power and
love: We rejoice with many of Thy people in celebrating this day
which commemorates Thy loving-kindness toward us and all men.
We praise Thy holy Name for purging the Church of its errors
and delivering it from the power of darkness. Accept again our
heartfelt thanks for bringing grace through the Bible and the holy
Sacraments; above all, we thank Thee for the direct way that has
been opened through the blood of our only Mediator and Saviour,
Christ Jesus our Lord. (66 ad)

REFORMATION PETITIONS AND INTERCESSIONS

With these mercies, O Triune God, grant to us a heart to love
Thee and to show forth Thy praise not only with our lips, but also
with our lives. Increase the faith and zeal of all Thy people. Make
us ready for large and fruitful work. Continue to enlighten, sanctify, and bless us through Thy Word and Sacraments. Preserve Thy
Church from doubt and impatience, from discouragement and discord. Revive the spirit of the Reformation in Thy Church that there
may be a larger outpouring of prayer, gifts, and personal service.
Give unto us a sincere willingness to take upon us the yoke of the
Christ and the duties that come to us as His followers. Endow Thy
servants with wisdom that the world-wide triumph of Thy Church
may be advanced. Defend us from all divisions, and unite us in the
bonds of a common faith and love. Hasten the promised day when
at the Name of Jesus every knee shall bow, and every tongue confess that He is Lord, to Thy glory. (66 ad)

FOR SCHOOLS, COLLEGES, AND UNIVERSITIES

Almighty God: We beseech Thee with Thy gracious favor to behold our universities, colleges, and other schools, that knowledge

may be increased among us, and all good learning flourish and abound. Bless all who teach and all who learn, and grant that in humility of heart they may ever look unto Thee, who art the Fountain of all wisdom. (128 ad)

For the Religious Press

O God, whose Word is a lamp for our feet and a light for our path: Grant wisdom, strength, and clearness of language to all who take up the pen to further the faith. Reassure them of Thy grace as they proclaim the good news through the printed page. Help them to keep aloft the torch of faith, that many may be encouraged to glorify Thee anew and walk in Thy ways. (109)

For the Battle of Life

Eternal God, who art a Refuge and Strength to Thy people: Protect us in the battle of life; gird us with truth, conviction, and purpose; help us to be ready to affirm the Gospel with our lips and lives; shield us in the true faith, that selfishness, pride, and jealousy may never overtake us; crown us with Thy salvation; and by the might of Thy Word empower us to remain faithful until the kingdom of darkness shall become the Kingdom of light. (109)

Communion of Saints

O Lord Most High: We give Thee thanks for all Thy saints, martyrs, and confessors; for all the faithful who in every age have witnessed a good confession, and have been the chosen vessels of Thy grace in their several generations. Grant us grace so to follow them as they followed Christ; and bring us, with them, to those things that eye has not seen, nor ear heard, which Thou hast prepared for those who love Thee. Through Jesus Christ our Lord, to whom with Thee and the Holy Spirit be all honor and glory, world without end. Amen. (128 ab)

Offertory Sentences and Prayer

1. He must reign until He has put all His enemies under His feet. *1 Cor. 15:25, R.S.V.*

2. "Go into all the world and preach the Gospel to the whole creation." *Mark 16:15, R.S.V.*

Accept, O Lord, these offerings Thy people make unto Thee, and grant that the cause to which they are devoted may prosper under Thy guidance, to the glory of Thy Name. Through Jesus Christ our Lord. Amen. (131)

49. WORLD ORDER SUNDAY (World Peace Sunday)

Usually celebrated on the Sunday nearest to October 24 or November 11.

Opening Sentences

1. Many nations shall come, and say, Come, and let us go up to the mountain of the Lord, and to the house of the God of Jacob; and He will teach us of His ways, and we will walk in His paths: for the law shall go forth of Zion, and the Word of the Lord from Jerusalem. *Micah 4:2.*

2. Righteousness exalteth a nation: but sin is a reproach to any people. *Prov. 14:34.*

3. They shall beat their swords into plowshares, and their spears into pruning hooks: nation shall not lift up a sword against nation, neither shall they learn war any more. *Micah 4:3.*

Invocation

All-wise God, who knowest our frame and our frailties: We invoke Thy presence and peace in this holy temple. Strengthen us, and all who seek Thy Kingdom, that we may be inspired to serve Thee in all walks of life. We beseech Thee to hasten the time when all men shall so worship Thee and honor Thy will that world order and peace may be established firmly among the family of nations. Through Thy Son, Jesus Christ, the Prince of Peace. Amen. (109)

Scripture Selections (129, 109)

O — *Ps.*	67	God Be Merciful to Us and Bless Us
Ps.	85	For God's Mercy on the Nation
Micah	*4:1–13*	Swords Into Plowshares
Matt.	*5:43–48*	Love to Enemies
Rom.	*12:17–21*	Overcoming Evil
Rom.	*13:1–7*	Subject to Higher Powers
II Tim.	*2:1–11*	A Good Soldier of Jesus

P — *Eph.*   6:10–20   The Christian Armor
  John   14:18–31   My Peace I Give Unto You
  Ps.   121   I Will Lift Up Mine Eyes

General Prayer

THANKSGIVING

Most heartily do we thank Thee, O Lord, for all Thy mercies of every kind, and for Thy loving care over all Thy creatures. We bless Thee for the gift of life, for Thy protection round about us, for Thy guiding hand upon us, and for the many tokens of Thy love within us; especially for the saving knowledge of Thy dear Son, our Redeemer, and for the living presence of Thy Spirit, our Comforter. We thank Thee for friendship and duty, for good hopes and precious memories, for the joys that cheer us, and for the trials that teach us to trust in Thee. In all these things, our Heavenly Father, make us wise in the right use of all Thy great benefits; and so direct us that in word and deed we may render an acceptable thanksgiving unto Thee. (129 ab)

FOR DELIVERANCE FROM SINS

Lord God Almighty: Defend our world, we beseech Thee, from the secret power and the open shame of great sins. From all dishonesty and disorder in the world, from all corruption and selfishness; from all cruelty and the spirit of violence; from all covetousness and impurity; and from intemperance, which is the mother of many crimes and sorrows, good Lord, deliver and save us, and our children, and our children's children. (127 ad)

Our Heavenly Father, in whose presence all disguises and pretenses do not avail: We acknowledge that the world's sin is our own, that the greed we condemn is in our heart; that the world is unjust because not one of us loves justice with sufficient abandon; that the vices of civilization are made up of the lusts of us all. Give us grace to look within our own hearts before we cast a stone of condemnation. (97 ad)

Bestow upon us the grace of true humility that we may cease to defeat Thy will for the world by our self-will. Help us to envision what we might be that we may be convicted of what we are. And let Thy mercy through Jesus Christ redeem us from our sin. (97 ad)

SPECIAL INTERCESSIONS
FOR MAIMED PATRIOTS

Heavenly Father: (On this anniversary of Armistice Day) We implore Thy gracious blessing on all maimed patriots, all widows and orphans of past wars. Grant that the memory of the sacrifices made in war may lead us to a greater dedication to the cause of world peace. (66 ad)

FOR WORLD PEACE

Inspire us with the spirit of the Prince of Peace. Cause the minds of men to enthrone Him in the councils of the mighty and the foreign policies of the nations. Strengthen the bonds of peace in all minds, in the ways of commerce and industry, governments and schools; in the dreams and imaginations of aspiring people, until swords are beaten into plowshares and the nations learn war no more. (66 and 99)

FOR MEN AND NATIONS

O God over all nations, whose will it is that all men may be drawn to Him who was lifted up: We pledge to Thee a renewed effort to bring men from all lands around the world to Thy Spirit, that they may glorify Thy Name. We consecrate ourselves anew to Thy love of the world, that the Gospel may be carried into the uttermost parts and all men live at peace with Thee and their fellow men. Bless the efforts of every agency engaged in the great task of proclaiming Thy will to all people. (145)

FOR THE UNITED NATIONS

Almighty and eternal God, Father of all peoples, who hast been our help in ages past and art our hope for years to come: Bless, we beseech Thee, the United Nations and all its work. Inspire its leaders and those who represent its members with the insight to understand, the courage to face boldly, and the patience to deal wisely with the disturbing problems of a world in peril. Deliver the nations from false pride and self-righteousness. Stir in their leaders and peoples the will to co-operate in the United Nations that, by Thy grace, we may establish peace with justice. Guide us to prepare in our communities and throughout the world for Thy eternal Kingdom of love and truth, of beauty and righteousness. (160 ad)

For Our Nation

Let Thy blessing rest on us as a nation. Enable every race which Thou hast drawn here to dedicate its noblest gifts to the common good. Hasten the day when the sense of kinship shall be firm and strong. Increase in us the will to do things that glorify Thee and uplift human hearts. Make us to be co-workers with Thee in establishing good will upon the earth. In Christ's Name. Amen. (100 ad)

Offertory Sentences and Prayer

1. And let us not be weary in well doing: for in due season we shall reap, if we faint not. *Gal. 6:9.*

2. Let us then pursue what makes for peace and for mutual upbuilding. *Rom. 14:19, R.S.V.*

O God, our Father: Be pleased to accept this offering of our money, the symbol of our love and devotion; and give Thy servants grace so to use it that Thy Name may be honored among men, and the happiness and prosperity of Thy Church increased. Through Jesus Christ our Lord. Amen. (55)

50. THANKSGIVING

The Fourth Thursday in November, or the Wednesday or
  Sunday Before
Color: Red (or White, 158)

Opening Sentences

1. O come, let us sing unto the Lord: let us make a joyful noise
to the Rock of our salvation. Let us come before His presence with
thanksgiving, and make a joyful noise unto Him with psalms. For
the Lord is a great God, and a great King above all gods. *Ps. 95:1–3.*

2. O give thanks unto the Lord; for He is good: for His mercy
endureth for ever. *Ps. 136:1.*

Invocation

Almighty God, our Heavenly Father: We thank Thee that Thou
hast bountifully blessed our country and nation, and dost continue
to enrich us with the gifts of Thy merciful goodness. Give us, we
beseech Thee, Thy Holy Spirit, that we may penitently, humbly, and
gratefully acknowledge Thy loving-kindness, and prepare ourselves
for the rewards to come in Thy everlasting Kingdom. Through
Jesus Christ our Lord. Amen. (66 and 127)

Scripture Selections (151, 66, 128)

A —	*Ps.*	*105:40–45*	God's Providential Care
	I Tim.	*2:1–8*	God Will Have All Men to Be Saved
P —	*Gal.*	*6:6–10*	Whatsoever a Man Soweth
	Luke	*12:13–34*	Be Not Anxious
	Ps.	*65*	God's Abundant Favor
S —	*Acts*	*17:22–31*	In Him We Live and Move and Have Our Being
	Luke	*12:15–21*	Parable of the Rich Man's Folly
	Matt.	*5:42–48*	God's Impartial Providence
	Deut.	*8:6–18*	Remember the Lord Your God

General Prayer

WE ADORE THEE

Lord God, eternal, sovereign, and immutable; holy, just, and merciful; Maker of all things by Thy power; Ruler of all things in Thy wisdom: We adore Thee for the wonders of the heavens and the earth; for the goodness of Thy dealings and the perfection of Thy ways; for Thy saving love revealed in Jesus Christ, and Thy living presence made known by the Holy Spirit. With voice and heart we offer unto Thee praise and adoration. (129 ab)

THANKS FOR MATERIAL BENEFITS

We adore Thee for the material benefits we have received. For the sunshine and the rain, for the fruits of the earth to minister to the needs of men, for food, clothing, and shelter, for the blessings of grace and protection that we have experienced, and for all friendly aid and encouragement that we have received, we offer unto Thee the sacrifice of our thanksgiving. (66 and 44)

HAVE MERCY

O Lord: We acknowledge our shortcomings and failures, and humbly confess our errors and sins. But forasmuch as Thou delightest to show mercy, we beseech Thee to pardon and absolve us, to deliver us from the burden of transgression, and to release us from the power of sin. (46)

SPECIAL INTERCESSIONS
IN A UNION SERVICE

Bless this union service of thanksgiving, O Heavenly Father. Help us to worship Thee in the beauty of holiness. Inspire us, that the words of our mouths and the meditations of our hearts may be acceptable in Thy sight, O Lord, our Rock and our Redeemer. Shower Thy blessings upon the churches represented here in the bonds of peace and fellowship. Continue to enrich and inspire the members of all churches everywhere, that as Thy children we may walk in brotherly love. (66 ad)

THANKS FOR THE DEPARTED FAITHFUL

O most loving Father: We remember with undying affection those near and dear to us whom death has taken away, and who rest from their earthly labors and sleep in Jesus. United still in one household of faith and love, help us to live in the blessed hope that when our day of departure shall come, we shall meet with them and all Thy redeemed in the glories of heaven. (27 ad)

FOR THE NATION

Most high and mighty Ruler of the universe: We thank Thee for Thy servants who established upon these shores a nation conceived in liberty and preserved in union. We pray that we citizens may so honor the memory of our forefathers that the Church and nation may stand in all the coming years for righteousness and peace.

Let Thy blessing rest upon Thy servant the President of the United States, and all who are in authority, and enable them to discharge the duties of their stations with wisdom and integrity. Grant unto them the spirit of true service. Keep us all in Thy care, and strengthen our hearts and hands that our work may redound to Thy glory.

And unto Thy great Name, the Father, the Son, and the Holy Spirit, we ascribe blessing, honor, and praise, now and forever. Amen. (66, 44, 48)

Offertory Sentences and Prayer

1. And whatever you do, in word or deed, do everything in the Name of the Lord Jesus, giving thanks to God the Father through Him. *Col. 3:17, R.S.V.*

2. None of us lives to himself. *Rom. 14:7, R.S.V.*

Almighty God, who inhabitest eternity, and yet makest Thyself known to us in countless ways: Receive, we beseech Thee, our offering, which we give as our humble expression of gratitude for Thy many blessings upon us and all mankind. In Jesus' Name. Amen. (109)

51. MEMORIAL SUNDAY
Last Sunday in the Church Year
Color: Black (or White, 147)

Or All Saints' Day
November 1
Color: Lutherans, Red; Episcopalians, White

For the Choir
O God of peace, who hast taught us that in returning and rest we shall be saved, in quietness and confidence shall be our strength: By the might of Thy Spirit lift us, we pray Thee, to Thy presence, where we may be still and know that Thou art God. Through Jesus Christ our Lord. Amen. (126)

Opening Sentences
Lord, Thou hast been our dwelling place in all generations. Before the mountains were brought forth, or ever Thou hadst formed the earth and the world, even from everlasting to everlasting, Thou art God. Thou turnest man to destruction; and sayest, Return, ye children of men. *Ps. 90:1–3.*

Invocation
O God, who makest Thyself known in the stillness: Let us feel Thy presence in this sacred place; make us to be of the company of brave saints who have worshiped here in spirit and in truth; through the voices of men and the instruments of praise give us to lift our hearts to Thee; and so, O Lord, purify our lives that, going forth into the world, we may go in Thy strength and in Thy love. Through Jesus Christ our Lord. Amen. (119 ad)

Scripture Selections (57)

A — *Rev.*	7:2–17	Robes Washed in the Blood of the Lamb	
Matt.	5:1–12	The Beatitudes	
O — *John*	11:11, 20–27	The Resurrection and the Life	

General Prayer

Praise for Those Who Were Faithful

Eternal God, our dwelling place in all generations: We would renew in this hour all fair and noble memories, all high and holy traditions of the days that are no more. We bless Thee for all the true and righteous souls who have revealed Thee to men, and who in their generation witnessed a good confession for the welfare of the world, whose memorial Thou hast set on high and whose names Thou hast made to shine as the stars forever.

Almighty Father, the God not of the dead but of the living: We have joy together in all our loved ones who have faithfully lived and peacefully died, and whose truth and beauty are even now in our hearts. May we be assured that they who are absent from us have found a more perfect rest in Thee, and the crown of our unfading life. Take the veil from our hearts, and join us in one communion with all Thy saints on earth and in heaven. (76)

Prayer of Humility

Let Thy beauty be upon us, O Lord, transforming our lives from what we are to that which we ought to be, uniting us in a new love, a new grace of service, and a new happiness of obedience. Make us to know that between us and Thee there is nothing but our own blindness of heart, since Thou art so near and we are often so far away. Make us one with all Thy seekers and finders, that at last we may be one with those who triumph over time and death by Thy grace. (95)

General Petitions

Eternal God: We bless Thee for the memory of the righteous and especially for those most dear to us, who lived in faith and departed in peace. May we follow their good example and be gathered with them into Thy heavenly Kingdom. (117)

Almighty God: We bless Thee for all the holy souls that reveal Thee, for all unknown and lowly people whose daily lives are offerings to Thee. Renew Thy call to us, and lift us into the liberty and joy of Thy faithful children. (117 ab)

O Thou who hast raised up prophets and apostles: Draw us unto Thyself by the same uplifting power, that our feet may not stumble in the dark mountains, nor falter in the valley of the shadow of death. (117)

Almighty God, who holdest in Thy hand the souls of the righteous: We bless Thee for those who have helped and defended us, and loved and cherished us. Grant that all the good we have felt and seen in them may continue to inspire and guide us; that we may always love them and hallow their memory. (117 ab)

Special Intercessions
For National Righteousness

O God, the Protector of all who put their trust in Thee: We pray for the good of our country, that it may please Thee to preserve to us the blessings of freedom. Unite in mutual understanding men of alien race and faith; revive in all hearts a spirit of devotion to the public good, that strife and tumult may be appeased and justice and truth be exalted. Enable us and all Thy people faithfully to discharge the duties of our different spheres, that the Kingdom of brotherhood and peace may be hastened upon the earth and Thy will be done even as now it is done in heaven. (117 ad)

For Loyalty

Teach us all, good Lord, to serve as Thou deservest; to give and not to count the wounds; to toil and not to seek for rest; to labor and not to ask for any reward, save of knowing that we do Thy will. Through Jesus Christ our Lord. Amen. (23)

Offertory Sentence and Prayer

For whosoever will save his life shall lose it: and whosoever will lose his life for My sake shall find it. *Matt. 16:25.*

All-gracious God, who of Thy infinite love didst give Thy only-begotten Son, Jesus Christ, to die for our sins and rise again for our justification, and hast made us partakers of the Divine nature through the gift of the Holy Spirit: Accept the offering which we now present unto Thee; and grant that our bodies, souls, and spirits may be unto Thee a living sacrifice, holy and well-pleasing in Thy sight; and that going forth in Thy strength, we may be able truly to serve Thee, and in all things to obey Thy will. Through Jesus Christ our Lord. Amen. (129)

52. UNIVERSAL BIBLE SUNDAY

Usually on the Second Sunday in December
Color: Purple

For the Choir

Open our lips, O Lord, that we may praise Thee; inspire our hearts that we may love Thee; and direct our thoughts that we may worship Thee. In praise and love and consecration teach us to glorify Thy Name. Amen. (72 ad)

Opening Sentences

1. The Lord is good unto them that wait for Him, to the soul that seeketh Him. *Lam. 3:25.*

2. Blessed are the undefiled in the way, who walk in the law of the Lord. Blessed are they that keep His testimonies, and that seek Him with the whole heart. *Ps. 119:1, 2.*

Invocation

O God, our Teacher, who through Thy Son hast taught us that they who continue in Thy Word shall know the truth which makes men free: Grant us such honesty in our study of Thy revelation of Thyself, that we may be delivered from the bondage of corruption into the glorious liberty of Thy children. Through Jesus Christ our Lord. Amen. (122 ad)

Scripture Selections (153, 152, 141)

O — *Ps.*	*119*	(Various Selections Suitable from the 176 Verses)
Jer.	*23:25-32*	Let Him Speak My Word Faithfully
Luke	*8:11-15*	Four Kinds of Ground for the Seed
John	*5:39-47*	Search the Scriptures
II Tim.	*3:15-17*	Scripture Is Profitable
Heb.	*4:12, 13*	The Word of God Is Powerful
I Peter	*1:17-25*	The Lord's Word Endureth Forever

General Prayer

ADORATION

Eternal and ever-blessed God: We bow down before Thy Divine majesty, adoring Thee, the Lord of heaven and earth, of whom and through whom and to whom are all things. Unto Thee be glory forever and ever. (124 ad)

THANKSGIVINGS, ESPECIALLY FOR THE BIBLE

For unnumbered mercies, often unnoticed and unimproved, and ever undeserved — all those temporal blessings Thou hast bestowed and the evils Thou hast averted — we thank and praise Thee. (124)

As for the blessings of Thy providence, so also would we thank Thee for the riches of Thy grace. For the ministry of Thy holy Son our Lord in word and deed, in life and death, reconciling the world unto Thyself; for the power and gifts of the Holy Spirit; and for the fellowship of the Church. (124 ab)

We rejoice and give thanks most especially this day for Thy Word, which Thou hast left unto us as a lamp unto our feet and a light unto our steps. Give unto us all Thy Holy Spirit, we humbly pray Thee, that out of the same Word we may learn what is Thy eternal will, and frame our lives in all holy obedience, to Thy honor and glory and the increase of our faith. (124 ad)

THE BLESSED HOPE

Blessed Lord, who hast caused all Holy Scriptures to be written for our learning: Grant that we may in such wise hear them, read, mark, learn, and inwardly digest them, that by patience and comfort of Thy holy Word we may embrace, and ever hold fast, the blessed hope of everlasting life, which Thou hast given us in our Saviour Jesus Christ. (126. Also the Collect in unit 2)

FOR AN ADVENT BLESSING

Conscious of our deep need for salvation from our sins and guidance into a life more like Thy Son's, we beseech Thee to strengthen us through Thy holy Word and Sacraments, that we might live acceptably in Thy sight. Graciously give ear unto our supplications as we cry out unto Thee for a new birth within! Help us to enthrone the Saviour in our hearts, that He may be first in our thoughts and desires, and that He may be to us, as He is to Thy angels, "Wonderful, Counselor, The mighty God, The everlasting Father, The Prince of Peace." (109)

FOR PEACE

Do Thou strengthen our efforts, and the efforts of Christians everywhere, that the powers of the world will recognize His government in righteousness and justice, and follow His example and establish foundations of peace among the nations of the earth, according to Thy holy Word and will. (109)

FOR THE SICK

Almighty and everlasting God, the Comfort of the sad, the Strength of those who suffer: Let the prayers of those who cry out of any tribulation come to Thee, that all may rejoice to find Thy mercy present with them in their affliction. (129 ad)

SPECIAL INTERCESSIONS
HEAR US

Hear us, O merciful Father, in these our intercessions and supplications, for the sake of Thy dear Son Jesus Christ, to whom, with Thee and the Holy Spirit, be all honor and glory, generation after generation. Amen. (66 ad)

Offertory Sentences and Prayer

And God is able to provide you with every blessing in abundance, so that you may always have enough of everything and may provide in abundance for every good work. As it is written, "He scatters abroad, He gives to the poor; His righteousness endures forever." *II Cor. 9:8, 9, R.S.V.*

Almighty God: Stir our hearts that by our prayers, our gifts, and our labors, we may have an ever greater part in the spreading of Thy Gospel over all the earth; and hasten the time when all the ends of the earth shall remember and turn unto Thee and all the people shall worship Thee. Through Jesus Christ our Lord. Amen. (105)

C. PRAYERS IN TIME OF WAR

For Guidance and Mercy

O Lord God, of infinite mercy: We beseech Thee to look in compassion upon our country now involved in war. Pardon our offenses, our pride and arrogance, our self-sufficiency and forgetfulness of Thee. Give wisdom to our counselors, skill to our officers, courage and endurance to our sailors, soldiers, and airmen, and all who guard our shores. Look in mercy on those immediately exposed to peril, conflict, sickness, and death. Be with the dying; give to them true repentance and unfeigned trust in Thee; and in the day of judgment, good Lord, deliver them. Finally, we beseech Thee to remove in Thy good providence all causes and occasions of war; to dispose our hearts and the hearts of our enemies to moderation; and of Thy great goodness, to restore peace among the nations. Through Christ our Lord. (46)

For Peace, and Deliverance from Our Enemies

O Almighty God, who art a strong tower of defense unto Thy servants against the face of their enemies: We yield Thee praise and thanksgiving for our deliverance from those great and apparent dangers wherewith we were compassed. We acknowledge it Thy goodness that we were not delivered over as a prey unto them; we beseech Thee still to continue such Thy mercies toward us, that all the world may know that Thou art our Saviour and mighty Deliverer. Through Jesus Christ our Lord. (126)

For Those in the Service

O God our Father: We commend to Thy keeping all the men and women serving our country by sea, land, and air, that we may win for the whole world the fruits of our sacrifice and a just peace. Through the grace of Jesus Christ our Lord. (128)

For Servicemen

O God: We especially implore Thy blessings upon those who have responded to our country's call to arms. Grant unto them the grace to obey willingly those who are in authority. Enable them, by the inspiration of Thy Holy Spirit, to find their lives in service to our country. Give them strength to carry on courageously until this war shall cease. If it be Thy will, help them to come back sound in body and mind. (109)

O Thou, who dost surely grieve over the iniquities of the children of men over all the earth: Have mercy upon us. Help us to learn the art of loving our neighbors consistently, that as a family of nations we may lead a quiet and tranquil life. Speed the day when world-wide brotherhood shall prevail and all hatred and greed shall be transformed into love and unselfish service through Thy redeeming power. In the Name of our Redeemer and Saviour, Jesus Christ, we humbly ask these petitions. (109)

For Service Men and Women

God of Grace: We pray for the young men and women who have left our midst for the armed forces of our country. Enable them to keep their visions fresh and their ideals high in these difficult times. Be with them, whether they are on land, on sea, or in the air.

Grant unto the leaders of our national life knowledge of Thy ways, good judgment between things more and things less important, that they may guide wisely whatever portion of destiny may be in their keeping. Knowing that their task in this hour of history is fraught with many perils, we unite in asking help from Thee that those who guide us may be guided by Thee.

We implore Thy comforting help for those from whom the young men and women in the service have been separated. Give abundant strength and courage with which to face this separation. Grant that, drawing nearer to Thee, they who are gone and we who are here may be bound together by Thy love in the communion of Thy Holy Spirit, and in the fellowship of Thy saints. Through Jesus Christ our Lord. (109)

When Servicemen Return

O Lord of heaven and earth, who art mindful of man and knowest what is in him: Graciously give ear to Thy people as we remember our relatives and friends returning from the armed forces of our country. As they return to our midst, may each note of joy contribute to a chorus of gratitude unto Thee. Direct our thoughts that in the spirit of unceasing devotion we may not forget those whom we have long remembered. Enable us to welcome our loved ones wisely. Give us grace to receive them with understanding. (109)

O God, who hast been a Refuge and Strength for Thy children even unto the ends of the earth: We implore Thy mercy especially upon those who have been wounded. Heal them, we pray Thee. Cause all who are sick in body, distressed in mind, or anxious in spirit to know that they are in Thy gracious care. Give a double portion of grace to those who feel the sting of unjust treatment. Grant unto all from the service a renewal of spirit, an upsurge of courage for life's difficulties and uncertainties, and the power to find their lives by losing themselves anew in service. Inspire them to live as unselfish servants in the great quest of rebuilding the world with Thee. Unite them with others around the globe in the arduous task of replacing hatred and greed with love and justice, through Thy transforming power. And unto Thee shall be the dominion forever and ever. (109)

A Prayer of Thanksgiving for Peace

Dear God: We thank Thee that recent efforts of various leaders have resulted in peace for a season. May the methods employed be used in establishing a firmer foundation for future peace. We ask Thee, O Lord, to bring peace and good will into the hearts of citizens of all countries involved in international difficulties. Restore that confidence and mutual understanding necessary for peaceful settlement of international crises. Then, finally, bring it to pass that we shall love one another even as Jesus Christ hath loved us. For this we most earnestly pray. Amen. (109)

Suggestion

Unit 49, World Order Sunday or World Peace Sunday, may be consulted also.

ACKNOWLEDGMENTS

For a book of this kind one is always immeasurably indebted to the Holy Spirit. This cannot be emphasized too much.

For concrete suggestions that have proved helpful in preparing this book, and for general suggestions on the material as a whole, I wish to thank Dr. Paul L. Meacham, Religious Book Editor of The Westminster Press, Dr. Purd E. Deitz, Bishop Ivan Lee Holt, and Dr. Deane Edwards.

I wish to acknowledge my gratitude to the following pastors who have helped with a revision of the body of this book: Rev. Samuel Martin, Rev. Kermit Olsen, Rev. E. H. Hammon.

The following others also gave suggestions for parts of the manuscript or on specific points within the manuscript: Professor C. R. Wylie, Rev. C. R. Jones, Rev. Harold Wilkie, the late Dr. R. E. Golladay, Dr. Herman Sweet, Dr. W. R. Grunewald, Rev. F. R. Stoneburner, Rev. Orville Cole, Rev. Ralph Parks, Rev. Theo. F. Schumacher, Rev. Herbert Kuhn, Miss Agnes Reeves, Rev. Chester H. Uthlaut, my three brothers, and my wife.

The following typed the manuscript through its six revisions: Mrs. Harry Todd, Miss Susanna B. Mayer, Miss Eunice Rohlfing, Mrs. Wilfred Kallmeyer, Mrs. Cecil Stancil, Miss Evelyn Zehr, and Mrs. Frank Vonderschmidt. Without the great aid of these helpers the manuscript could not have been prepared in its present form.

I am greatly indebted to the numerous sources of great prayers. For certain occasions the problem was to select only one of many outstanding prayers, or to select one of several revised forms of outstanding ancient prayers. For other parts of the manuscript new prayers had to be written.

A book, now out of print, that I found particularly valuable as a source of materials was the *Evangelical Book of Worship*. Prayers were freely adapted from this book, which, strangely, had but a limited circulation. While I also feel greatly indebted to the thirty-odd sources to each of which I have referred four or more times, I feel very grateful to many of the sources from which only one good prayer was taken. Many of the most familiar prayers can be found in other books as well as the ones to which reference happens to be given.

An attempt was made to list all sources accurately. Information concerning a mistake in giving credit, or an infringement of copyright, will be gratefully received and noted for possible future editions or enlargements of this book.

For permission to quote and adapt recent material, we acknowledge our gratitude to the following publishers, individuals, and committees:

Abingdon-Cokesbury Press: Carl A. Glover, *The Lectern: A Book of Public Prayers.* Copyright, 1946, by Stone & Pierce.

Owen G. Barrow: A prayer in the May, 1948, issue of *The Pulpit Digest.*

The Beacon Press: *Services for Congregational Worship.* American Unitarian Association.

Paul C. Bloesch: Two forms for the confession of sin.

Donald Cameron: Hugh Cameron, *Prayers for Use in Public Worship.* Alexander Brunton.

Central Publishing House: *Book of Worship* of the Evangelical and Reformed Church, 1940 and 1947 editions; *The Book of Worship for the Reformed Church in the U. S.;* and J. Storrer, *Compendium of Biblical Texts and Topics for Every Sunday of the Year.*

The Church of Scotland, Committee on Public Worship and Aids to Devotion: *Prayers for the Christian Year,* Oxford University Press; *The Book of Common Order* of the Church of Scotland, Oxford University Press.

James Clarke & Co., Ltd.: Hubert L. Simpson, *Let Us Worship God.*

The Congregational Christian Churches, the Board of Home Missions: *A Book of Worship for Free Churches.* Oxford University Press.

J. M. Dent & Sons, Ltd.: William Angus Knight, *Prayers Ancient and Modern.*

E. P. Dutton & Co., Inc.: John Hunter, *Devotional Services for Public Worship;* Selina Fitzherbert Fox, *A Chain of Prayer Across the Ages;* Wilbur Thirkield and Oliver Huckel, *Book of Common Worship;* William E. Orchard, *The Temple.*

Mrs. Lisgar R. Eckardt: Lisgar R. Eckardt, a prayer in *The Book of Worship for Church and Home.* The Methodist Publishing House.

Evangelical and Reformed Church, Continuation Committee of the Evangelical Synod of North America: *Evangelical Book of Worship.* Eden Publishing House.

Fiduciary Trust Co. of Boston and Mrs. Charles Lewis Slattery: Bishop Charles Lewis Slattery, *Prayers for Private and Family Use.* The Macmillan Company.

Federal Council of the Churches of Christ in America, the Commission on Worship: Mark Rich, *Rural Life Prayers.*

The First Congregational Church, Webster Groves, Missouri: A short creed.

Edward G. Fischer: Francis Greenwood Peabody, *Prayers for Various Occasions and Needs.* Houghton Mifflin Co.

The Friendship Press: Henry van Dyke, in Diffendorfer, *Thy Kingdom Come.*

Goodenough & Woglom Co.: William H. Leach, *The Days We Observe.*

Harold C. Grunewald: A poem used on the Fourth Sunday in Lent.

The International Council of Religious Education: *Revised Standard Version of the New Testament* and *The American Standard Edition of the Revised Bible.*

Howard Kelsey: A prayer used on Palm Sunday.

P. J. Kenedy & Sons: Charles J. Callan and John A. McHugh, *The Catholic Missal.*

Jackson, Son & Co.: *Service Book and Ordinal of the Presbyterian Church of South Africa.*

William H. Leach: J. Richmond Morgan, prayers in December, 1938, issue of *Church Management.*

Longmans, Green & Co., Inc.: Henry Sylvester Nash, *Prayers and Meditations.*

A. William Loos, Education Secretary of The Church Peace Union: A prayer for the United Nations.

The Macmillan Company: Walter Russell Bowie, *Lift Up Your Hearts;* Albert W. Palmer, *Aids to Worship; Acts of Devotion.*

Elmore M. McKee and Harper and Brothers: Elmore M. McKee, *Communion with God.* Ray Long and Richard R. Smith, Inc.

The Methodist Publishing House: *The Book of Worship for Church and Home.* Copyright, 1944, 1945, by Whitmore & Stone.

Morehouse-Gorham Co.: Frank E. Wilson, *An Outline of Christian Symbolism,* and *An Outline of the Christian Year; A Book of Offices and Prayers for Priest and People.* Edwin S. Gorham, Inc.

Oxford University Press, Inc.: *The Kingdom, the Power and the Glory,* an American Edition of *The Grey Book.* Copyright, 1933, by Oxford University Press, Inc.; William E. Orchard, *The Order of Divine Service for Public Worship.*

The Pilgrim Press: Henry Hallam Saunderson, *Pulpit and Parish Manual;* Charles Wolcott Merriam, *Church Worship Book;* Charles H. Richards, Chairman, *Book of Church Services;* Walter Rauschenbusch, *Prayers of the Social Awakening.*

The Presbyterian Church in Canada: *The Book of Common Order* of the Presbyterian Church in Canada. Presbyterian Publications, Toronto.

The Presbyterian Church in Ireland, Public Worship Committee: *A Book of Orders for Public Worship* of the Presbyterian Church in Ireland. Graham and Heslip, Ltd., The Franklin Works.

Presbyterian Church of England, Publications Committee: John Watson, *Prayers and Services.*

Reformed Church in America, the Board of Education: *The Liturgy of the Reformed Church in America.* The Board of Publications.

Fleming H. Revell Company: Charles Morris Addison, *Prayers for the Christian Year.* The Century Company.

Rivingtons, London: Percy Dearmer, *The Sanctuary.*

Charles Scribner's Sons: Morgan Phelps Noyes, *Prayers for Services;* Burton Scott Easton and Howard Chandler Robbins, *The Eternal Word in the Modern World.*

S.P.C.K., London: J. S. Hoyland, *A Book of Prayers.* The Challenge Books and Pictures, Ltd.

John Wallace Suter and Harper and Brothers: John Wallace Suter, *Prayers of the Spirit*.

J. M. Lloyd Thomas: *A Free Book of Common Prayer*. J. M. Dent and Sons.

The United Church of Canada and The Ryerson Press: *The Book of Common Order* of the United Church of Canada. United Church Publishing House, Toronto.

The United Lutheran Church in America: *Common Service Book of the Lutheran Church*.

The United Lutheran Publication House: Paul Zeller Strodach, *Oremus — Collects, Devotions, Litanies from Ancient and Modern Sources;* Paul Zeller Strodach, *A Manual on Worship*, Muhlenberg Press; Charles Michael Jacobs, *Helps on the Road*. Board of Publication of the United Lutheran Church.

Charles L. Wallis and Harper and Brothers: James Dalton Morrison, *Minister's Service Book*. Willett, Clark, and Co.

Charles L. Wan: *Book of Common Order of St. Giles' Cathedral*.

The Woolverton Printing Company: Two offertory prayers from their bulletins.

SOURCES

The numbers in parentheses after specific items in the body of this book refer to the sources and publishers.

Where only a portion of a prayer was used, but not changed, the letters *ab* for " abridgment " were placed after the reference number. Where an adaptation was made, the letters *ad* were placed after the reference number. Quite often several adaptations were made in the prayers so indicated, but leaders of worship may want to adapt the prayers still more, or make substitutions in places.

Where a prayer was adapted with phrases from another prayer, two source numbers are listed after the prayer. Occasionally parts of three prayers were combined, in which case three reference numbers are listed.

Attention may be called to the reasons for adapting much of the material. For one thing, it was my purpose at all times to present material according to a pattern that was thought to be most useful in the local church. Instead of merely copying one prayer after another, I endeavored to eliminate any unnecessary repetition of thought. For example, the General Prayer for the unit of thanksgiving materials could easily have contained more than one prayer of thanksgiving for food, clothing, and shelter. In a similar manner many well-worded prayers were abridged or adapted when incorporated into the framework of the General Prayers throughout the book. Another thought that made adaptation necessary was the conviction that educational features in a prayer should be minimized as much as possible. An example of what we mean by an " educational feature " could be a prayer something like this:

" This is Palm Sunday. This is the day that Jesus rode triumphantly into the city of Jerusalem as children cried, saying, ' Hosanna; Blessed is He that cometh in the Name of the Lord.' "

We preferred the following form for prayer:

" O Lord, we praise Thee for the Master who rode in triumph into

the city of His fathers. We thank Thee that He came not as a conqueror to destroy, but as the Messiah to save." (90 ab)

I

Ancient and Old Sources (Before a.d. 1800)

1. *An Ancient Abyssinian Jacobite Liturgy.*
2. Andrewes, Bishop Lancelot. a.d. 1555.
3. Augustine, Saint, *Confessions of St. Augustine.* 4th Century.
4. Calvin, John. 16th Century.
5. *Coptic Liturgy of St. Basil.* 4th Century.
6. *Coptic Liturgy of St. Cyril.* a.d. 315.
7. *Eastern Church Liturgy; Day-break Office.* 3d Century.
8. *Gallican Sacramentary.* a.d. 354.
9. *Gelasian Sacramentary.* a.d. 494.
10. Greek Church Liturgy, Source No. 18.
11. *Gregorian Sacramentary.* a.d. 590.
12. Hamilton, Archbishop. a.d. 1511.
13. Hawkins, Canon E. a.d. 1789.
14. Irenaeus, Bishop. a.d. 170.
15. Kempis, Thomas a. a.d. 1379.
16. Laud, Archbishop William. a.d. 1573.
17. *Leonine Sacramentary.* a.d. 440.
18. *Liturgy of the Greek Church.* 3d Century.
19. *Liturgy of Malabar.* 5th Century.
20. *Liturgy of St. Chrysostom.* a.d. 398.
21. *Liturgy of St. James.* 2d Century.
22. *Liturgy of St. Mark.* a.d. 175.
23. Loyola, Ignatius. 16th Century.
24. *Mozarabic Liturgy.* Before a.d. 700.
25. Taylor, Jeremy. *Free Church Book of Common Prayer.* Edinburgh. 17th Century.
26. *The Scottish Psalter.* a.d. 1595.

II

SOURCES AFTER A.D. 1800

27. *A Book of Common Order*. Fifth Edition, Revised and Enlarged. The Church Service Society. William Blackwood and Sons, Edinburgh and London, 1884.

28. *A Book of Offices and Prayers for Priest and People*. Compiled by two presbyters of the Church. Edwin S. Gorham, Inc., New York, 1927.

29. *A Book of Orders for Public Worship* of the Presbyterian Church in Ireland. Graham and Heslip, Ltd., Belfast, 1942.

30. *A Book of Worship for Free Churches*. Prepared under the direction of the General Council of the Congregational Christian Churches in the United States. Oxford University Press, New York, 1948.

31. *A Bulletin for National Missions*. Issued by the Board of National Missions of the Evangelical and Reformed Church, Philadelphia and St. Louis.

32. *A Church Service Book*, quoted in Morrison, *Minister's Service Book*.

33. *A Free Book of Common Prayer*. J. M. Dent and Sons, Ltd., London.

34. *A Guide for the Christian Year*. Seminar on Worship, Congregational Churches, Commission on Evangelism and Devotional Life. New York City.

35. *A New Directory for the Public Worship of God*. Prepared by the then Free Church of Scotland. Macniven and Wallace, Edinburgh, 1898.

36. "A Service of Worship for the Festival of the Christian Home," prepared by the Commission on Worship of the Federal Council of the Churches of Christ, New York, 1945.

37. *Acts of Devotion*. The Macmillan Company, New York, 1927.

38. Addison, Charles Morris, *Prayers for the Christian Year*. The Century Company, New York, 1931.

39. Alford, Henry, *The Year of Prayer*. Alex Stracham, London and New York, 19th Century.

40. Bensen, Archbishop. A.D. 1829. In Fox's *A Chain of Prayer Across the Ages.*

41. Bensen, R. M., *Intercessory Manual.* 1875. In Fox's *A Chain of Prayer Across the Ages.*

42. Benson, Louis F., *A Book of Family Worship.* Presbyterian Board of Publication, Philadelphia, 1921.

43. Bloesch, Paul C.

44. *Book of Church Services.* Prepared by a Commission of the National Council of Congregational Churches, Charles H. Richards, Chairman. The Pilgrim Press, Boston, 1932.

45. *Book of Common Order.* Issued by the Church Service Society. William Blackwood & Sons, Edinburgh and London. Sixth Edition, 1890.

46. *The Book of Common Order* of the Church of Scotland. Oxford University Press. Glasgow, Edinburgh, London, et cetera, 1940.

47. *Book of Common Order of St. Giles' Cathedral.* Edinburgh, 1922.

48. *Book of Common Worship.* For use in the Several Communions of the Church of Christ. Bishop Wilbur Thirkield and The Rev. Oliver Huckel, Editors. E. P. Dutton & Co., Inc., New York, 1932.

49. *Book of Worship.* General Synod of the Evangelical and Reformed Church. Central Publishing House, Cleveland, 1940.

50. *Book of Worship.* General Synod of the Evangelical and Reformed Church. Revised and Enlarged Edition. Central Publishing House, Cleveland, 1947.

51. Bright, William, *Ancient Collects.* James Parker and Co., Oxford and London. Compiled in 1875.

52. Bowie, Walter Russell, *Lift Up Your Hearts.* The Macmillan Company, New York, 1939.

53. Cameron, Hugh, *Prayers for Use in Public Worship.* Alexander Brunton, Edinburgh, 1921.

54. *Church Book for the Use of Evangelical Lutheran Congregations.* J. K. Shryock, Philadelphia, 1893.

55. Cleaves, Arthur W., in Morrison's *Minister's Service Book.*

56. Coffin, Henry Sloane, in Noyes's *Prayers for Services.* Com-

bined with a prayer from *Anthology of Prayers for Public Worship,* issued by the Church Worship Association of the United Free Church of Scotland. Macniven and Wallace, Edinburgh, 1907. The prayers in unit 21 are adapted from Coffin. The prayer in unit 43 is mostly from *Anthology of Prayers.*

57. *Common Service Book of the Lutheran Church.* The General Synod of the Evangelical Lutheran Church in the U. S. A., The Trustees of the General Council of the Evangelical Lutheran Church in N. A., and the United Synod of the Evangelical Lutheran Church in the South, 1917. The collect in unit 27 was written by Thomas Aquinas.

58. Coulburn, Dean. 19th Century. In Fox's *A Chain of Prayer Across the Ages.*

59. Dawson, George A., *A Collection of Prayers.* Kegan Paul, Trench, Trubner & Co., London. Ninth Edition, 1885.

60. Dearmer, Percy, *The Sanctuary.* Rivingtons, London, 1905.

61. *Devotional Offices for General Use.* In Morrison's *Minister's Service Book.*

62. Diffendorfer, Ralph Eugene, *Thy Kingdom Come.* Missionary Education Movement, New York, 1914.

63. *Directory and Forms for Public Worship.* Church Worship Association of the United Free Church of Scotland. Macniven and Wallace, Edinburgh, 1909.

64. Eckhardt, Lisgar R., in the Methodist *Book of Worship for Church and Home.*

65. Ellis, Rufus, *Prayers.* W. B. Clarke and Carruth, Boston, 1886.

66. *Evangelical Book of Worship.* Published by the German Evangelical Synod of North America. Eden Publishing House, St. Louis and Chicago, 1916.

67. *Farnham Hostel Manual of Prayers.* 19th Century. In Noyes's *Prayers for Services.*

68. First Congregational Church, Webster Groves, Missouri. From a bulletin.

69. Fisher, A. S. T., *An Anthology of Prayers.* Compiled for use in school and home. Longmans, Green & Co., London, New York, Toronto, 20th Century.

70. Fitch, Albert Parker. Quoted in Noyes's *Prayers for Services.*

71. Fox, Selina Fitzherbert, *A Chain of Prayer Across the Ages.* E. P. Dutton and Company, Inc., New York, 1913.

72. Glover, Carl A., *The Lectern: A Book of Public Prayers.* Abingdon-Cokesbury Press, New York and Nashville, 1946.

73. Grunewald, Harold C.

74. Hoben, A., in McComb's *A Book of Modern Prayers,* Longmans, Green & Co., New York, 1926.

75. Hoyland, J. S., *A Book of Prayers.* Written for use in an Indian college. The Challenge Books and Pictures, Ltd., London, 1921.

76. Hunter, John, *Devotional Services for Public Worship.* E. P. Dutton and Co., Inc., New York. J. M. Dent and Sons, London. Ninth Edition, 1915.

77. Jacobs, Charles Michael, *Helps on the Road.* Board of Publications of the United Lutheran Church in America, Philadelphia.

78. Jones, R. C., *A Book of Prayers.* Williams and Norgate, London, 19th Century.

79. Kelsey, Howard.

80. King, Bishop Edward. 1829. Quoted in Fox, *A Chain of Prayer.*

81. Knight, William Angus, *Prayers Ancient and Modern.* J. M. Dent & Sons, London, 19th Century.

82. Ledden, W. Earl. Quoted in Morrison's *Minister's Service Book.*

83. Lotz, P. Henry, *The Quest for God Through Worship.* The Bethany Press, St. Louis.

84. Lowell, James Russell.

85. Macy, Paul Griswold, in *A Book of Worship for Free Churches.*

86. *Manual of Prayers for Unity,* quoted in *Free Church Book of Common Prayer.*

87. Martin, Sir William. 19th Century. Quoted in Fox, *A Chain of Prayer.*

88. Martineau, James, *Home Prayers.* Longmans, Green & Co., London and New York, 1891.

89. McKee, Elmore M., *Communion with God.* Ray Long and Richard R. Smith, Inc., New York, 1932.

90. Merriam, Charles Wolcott, *Church Worship Book*. The Pilgrim Press, Boston and Chicago, 1931.

91. Morrison, James Dalton, *Minister's Service Book* for Pulpit and Parish Use. Willett, Clark and Co., Chicago and New York. Third printing, 1937.

92. Myers, A. J. William, *Enriching Worship*. Harper and Brothers, New York, 1949.

93. Nash, Henry Sylvester, *Prayers and Meditations*. Longmans, Green & Co., London and New York, 19th Century.

94. Newman, John Henry.

95. Newton, Joseph Fort, quoted in Palmer's *Aids to Worship*.

96. Newton, Joseph Fort, quoted in *Service Book and Ordinal of the Presbyterian Church of South Africa*.

97. Niebuhr, Reinhold, in Noyes's *Prayers for Services*.

98. Novotny, Louise Miller, *Special Days in the Church School*. The Standard Publishing Company, Cincinnati, 1943.

99. Noyes, Morgan Phelps, *Prayers for Services*. Charles Scribner's Sons, New York, London, 1935. Helpful also in finding many other excellent aids.

100. *Old Joint Synod of Ohio Liturgy*. Lutheran Book Concern, Columbus.

101. Orchard, William E., *The Order of Divine Service for Public Worship*. Compiled from Ancient and Modern Devotions. Oxford University Press, London, New York, etc., 1921.

102. Orchard, William E., *The Temple*. Copyrighted by E. P. Dutton & Co., Inc., New York. J. M. Dent & Sons, London, 1913.

103. Palmer, Albert W., *Aids to Worship*. The Macmillan Company, New York, 1944.

104. Peabody, Francis Greenwood, *Prayers for Various Occasions and Needs*. Houghton Mifflin Company, Boston and New York, 1930.

105. *Prayers for Divine Services*. Scotch Presbyterian. William Blackwood & Sons, Edinburgh.

106. *Prayers for Individuals and Families*. Evangelical Lutheran Synod of Ohio and Other States. Lutheran Book Concern, Columbus, Ohio, 1888.

107. *Prayers for the Christian Year*. Prepared by a Committee of

the Church of Scotland. Oxford University Press, Glasgow, Edinburgh, London, New York, etc., 1935.

108. Rauschenbusch, Walter, *Prayers of the Social Awakening*. The Pilgrim Press, Boston, 1909.

109. Rest, Friedrich.

110. Rich, Mark, *Rural Life Prayers*. Commission on Worship of the Federal Council of the Churches of Christ in America, New York, Second Edition, Revised, 1943.

111. " Rural Life Sunday, 1930," in Rich's *Rural Life Prayers*.

112. Rossetti, Christina G. 19th Century.

113. Saunderson, Henry Hallam, *Pulpit and Parish Manual*. The Pilgrim Press, Boston, Chicago, 1930.

114. Scudamore, W. E. 1850.

115. Selzer, George R.

116. *Service Book and Ordinal of the Presbyterian Church of South Africa*. Jackson, Son & Co., Glasgow. Second Edition, 1929.

117. *Services for Congregational Worship*. American Unitarian Association. The Beacon Press, Inc., Boston, 1914.

118. Simpson, Hubert L., *Let Us Worship God*. James Clarke & Co., London, 1928.

119. Slattery, Bishop Charles Lewis, *Prayers for Private and Family Use*. The Macmillan Company, New York, 1922.

120. Strodach, Paul Zeller, *Oremus — Collects, Devotions, Litanies from Ancient and Modern Sources*. Board of Publications of the United Lutheran Church in America, Philadelphia, 1935.

121. Suter, John Wallace, *Devotional Offices for General Use*. The Century Co., 1928.

122. Suter, John Wallace, *Prayers of the Spirit*. Harper & Brothers, New York and London, 1943.

123. *The Book of Common Order* of the Church of Scotland. By Authority of the General Assembly. Oxford University Press, Edinburgh, Glasgow, London, etc., 1940.

124. *The Book of Common Order* of the Presbyterian Church in Canada. Presbyterian Publications, Toronto, 1938. Second Revised Edition, 1948.

125. *The Book of Common Order* of the United Church of Canada. United Church Publishing House, Toronto, 1932.

126. *The Book of Common Prayer*. According to the Use of the Protestant Episcopal Church in the U. S. A. Revised Edition, Oxford University Press, 1932.

127. *The Book of Common Worship*. The Board of Christian Education of the Presbyterian Church in the U. S. A., Philadelphia. Revised, 1932.

128. *The Book of Common Worship*. The Board of Christian Education of the Presbyterian Church in the U. S. A., Philadelphia. Revised. Copyright, 1946.

129. *The Book of Common Worship*. The Presbyterian Board of Publication and Sabbath-School Work, Philadelphia, 1906.

130. *The Book of Worship for the Reformed Church in the U. S.* The Publication and Sunday School Board of the Reformed Church in the U. S., Philadelphia, 1926.

131. *The Book of Worship for Church and Home*. The Methodist Publishing House, 1944, 1945.

132. *The Catholic Missal,* Being a Translation of the " New Missale Romanum " Arranged for Daily Use. Charles J. Callan and John A. McHugh, editors. P. J. Kenedy & Sons, New York. Revised, 1943.

133. *The Kingdom, the Power and the Glory*. Services of Praise and Prayer for Occasional Use in Churches. An American Edition of *The Grey Book,* Oxford University Press, New York, 1933.

134. " The Every Member Canvass." Quoted in Morrison's *Minister's Service Book*.

135. *The Liturgy of the Reformed Church in America,* Together with *The Psalter*. The Board of Publications of the Reformed Church in America, New York, 1907 copyright, 1950 edition.

136. *The Rugby Office*. Quoted in Noyes, *Prayers for Services*.

137. *Treasury of Devotion*. 1872. Quoted in Fox, *A Chain of Prayer*.

138. *Twenty-five Consecration Prayers*. A. Linton. S.P.C.K., 1921.

139. Unknown Source.

140. Van Dyke, Henry, in Diffendorfer, *Thy Kingdom Come*.

141. Wagner, James, " A Series of Six Stewardship Devotional Services." Committee on Stewardship of the General Council of the Evangelical and Reformed Church, Philadelphia, 1946.

142. Watson, John, *Prayers and Services*. Publications Committee, Presbyterian Church of England, London, 1909.

143. Westcott, Bishop Brook Foss, *Prayers for Family Use*. The Macmillan Co., London, 1825.

144. *Westminster Prayers,* P. Dearmer and F. R. Barry. Oxford University Press, 1936.

145. Wilson, Warren H., in *Year Book of Prayer for Missions.* The Presbyterian Church in the U.S.A., New York, 1930.

III

Supplementary Sources (Related Books, Magazines, etc.)

146. Barrow, Owen G., in *Pulpit Digest,* May, 1948, issue. Great Neck, New York.

147. *Evangelical and Reformed Year Book — 1951.* Board of Business Management of the Evangelical and Reformed Church, Philadelphia, Cleveland, St. Louis, 1950.

148. *Evangelical Catechism.* Evangelical Synod of North America. Eden Publishing House, St. Louis, 1929.

149. Leach, William H., *The Days We Observe.* Goodenough and Woglom Co., New York, 1943.

150. Morgan, J. Richmond, in *Church Management,* December, 1938, issue. Cleveland.

151. Nesper, Paul W., *Biblical Texts for Special Occasions.* Lutheran Book Concern, Columbus, 1923.

152. Notkin, Louis, *The Quotable Bible.* Samuel Curl, Inc., New York, 1941.

153. Parker, Eric, *Anthology of the Bible.* J. B. Lippincott Company, Philadelphia, 1940.

154. Soll, Frederic H. K., *Pericopes and Selections.* Published by the author. Yakima, Washington, 1929.

155. Storrer, J., *Compendium of Biblical Texts and Topics for Every Sunday of the Year.* Central Publishing House. The range of Church year dates throughout this book are taken from Storrer's book.

156. Strodach, Paul Zeller, *A Manual on Worship.* Revised Edition. Muhlenberg Press, Philadelphia, 1946.

157. *The Eternal Word in the Modern World,* Burton Scott Easton and Howard Chandler Robbins. Charles Scribner's Sons, New York and London, 1937.

158. Wilson, Frank E., *An Outline of Christian Symbolism.* Morehouse-Gorham Co., N. Y., 1938, and *An Outline of the Christian Year.* Morehouse-Gorham, 1944.

159. Woolverton Press, 1938. From a bulletin by the Press in Cedar Falls, Iowa.

IV

ADDITIONAL SOURCES

(Too late to be included in the alphabetical arrangement)

160. Loos, A. William, in a pamphlet, *United Nations Week, Oct. 16–24, 1950,* published by The Church Peace Union and the World Alliance for International Friendship Through Religion. New York, 1950.

161. *A Book of Orders for Public Worship* of the Presbyterian Church in Ireland. By Authority of the General Assembly. Graham and Heslip Ltd., The Franklin Works, Belfast, 1942.

INDEX

(According to Units, not Pages)